Nancy Cornwell's

More Polar Magic

Expanded Fleece Techniques

©2004 Nancy Cornwell

Published by

An F+W Publications Company

700 East State Street • Iola, WI 54990-0001
715-445-2214 • 888-457-2873
www.krause.com

Our toll-free number to place an order or obtain
a free catalog is (800) 258-0929.

The following product and company names appear in this book:

Chenille by the Inch™ (Fabric Café™), Chacopel Pencils (Clover Needlecraft, Inc.), Cambridge Marking System, Do-Sew® (Stretch & Sew, Inc.), Electric Scissors (Prym-Dritz Corp.), Fasturn® Tube Turner (Crowning Touch, Inc.), Faux Chenille™ (Nanette Holmberg), Hello Kitty® (San Rio Co., Ltd.), Husqvarna (Viking Sewing Machines, Inc.), L'Orna® Decorative Touch™ (Kandi Corp.), Lycra™ (DuPont Co.), Mesh Transfer Canvas (Clover Needlecraft, Inc.), Mini Iron™ (Clover Needlecraft, Inc.), Nancy's Notions® (Nancy's Notions, Ltd.), Nordic Fleece™ (David Textiles, Inc.), Olfa® (Olfa-North America), Omnistrips™ (Omnigrid®, Inc.), Pellon® Quilter's Grid™ (Freudenberg Nonwovens), Polarfleece® (Malden Mills Industries, Inc.), Polartec® (Malden Mills Industries, Inc.), Shape Cut™ from Quiltools™ (June Tailor), Shape Cut™ Plus from Quiltools™ (June Tailor), Solar™ Fleece (Siltex Mills, Ltd.), Staple Sewing Aids Corp., Stitch Effects Iron-On Transfers™ (Delta Technical Coatings, Inc.), Sulky® KK2000™ (Gunold + Stykma), Sulky® Ultra Solvy™ (Gunold + Stykma), Swarovski® (Daniel Swarovski & Co.), Teflon® (DuPont Co.), UltraSuede® (Toray UltraSuede® America, Inc.), Velcro® (Velcro Industries B.V.), Viking Sewing Machines, Inc., Wash-Away Wonder Tape (W.H. Collins, Inc.), Water-Soluble Pencils (Clover Needlecraft, Inc.), Yukon Fleece™ (Huntingdon Mills Ltd.)

Library of Congress Catalog Number: 2004092859

ISBN: 0-87349-810-0

Edited by Barbara Case
Designed by Marilyn McGrane
Printed in the United States

Dedication

To my husband Jeff
who, as always, offers
me constant support,
encouragement, and
understanding in all my
endeavors.

Acknowledgments

It takes more than ideas and creativity to create a book. It takes supportive companies who continually provide quality products that enable ideas to blossom into reality. It is those companies and people I would like to acknowledge here.

My heartfelt thanks go to:

David Textiles, Inc.

For their high quality Nordic Fleece line. Their phenomenal prints and broad range of luscious colors keep the home sewer's creative energy charged and make sewing a joy.

Nancy Zieman

For all she has done for our industry. She is truly the heart of the home sewing industry. I especially thank the "other Nancy" for writing the Foreword for this book.

Sue Hausmann and Viking Sewing Machines, Inc.

Sue does a terrific job to "Keep America Sewing." I appreciate the continual support of the Viking Sewing Machine Co. in constantly providing me with product and information to keep my ideas flowing.

Sulky of America

For listening and responding to sewer's requests. For giving us the tools necessary to attempt innovative techniques our machines and fabrics were never intended to do.

Clover Needlecraft, Inc.

Especially Jan Carr and Syl Pierson for continually keeping me "in the loop" with new products, techniques, and ideas that spark new fleece ideas. I particularly thank Clover for their mesh transfer canvas and water-soluble pencils. Those tools make transferring designs onto fleece a breeze.

Prym-Dritz Corp.

Especially Dianne Giancola for supplying product and information to help me create new fleece adventures.

Credit:

Most of the garments and blankets featured in this book were made using Nordic Fleece manufactured by David Textiles, Inc. I chose this fleece because I can count on its consistent high quality and know it is readily available through all fabric shops. If your local fabric store doesn't carry Nordic Fleece, ask the owner or manager to order it.

Foreword
by Nancy Zieman

When I think of Polarfleece, I automatically think of Nancy Cornwell. And as the "other Nancy," it is my pleasure to write the foreword to Nancy's newest book. As a resident of Wisconsin, I can definitely appreciate the comfort and appeal of fleece. Nancy Cornwell succeeds in transforming this fabric into amazing creations, using a variety of techniques.

My reaction to *More Polar Magic* is best summed up in one phrase, "Why didn't I think of that?" In this, Nancy's latest adventure in fleece, she takes us on a wonderful journey, exploring the creative possibilities of working with fleece.

This book inspires you to think outside of the box. I love that! Nancy has designed many wonderful fleece projects. However, she does not expect you to simply follow her instructions and call it a day. Nancy's unique way of teaching encourages you to explore the possibilities in each of these techniques, letting them evolve into new and exciting projects.

Discover the joy of sewing with fleece!

After taping for the television program, *Sewing With Nancy*, Nancy C. showed Nancy Z. how she created the chenille sleeves for the Jaguar Jacket.

Table of Contents

Chapter 1: Quick Refresher Course 9

Nancy's Golden Rules..................................... 10

Fabric Basics 13

General Sewing Basics................................... 14

Chapter 2: Gotta-Have Notions............................ 16

References 17

Notions.. 18

Chapter 3: Blunt Edge Finish............................22

Single-Layer – Lapped Seams and Patchwork................ 23

    Patchwork Embroidered Quilt........................... 23

    Patchwork Scarf...24

    Patchwork Jacket... 26

Double-Layer – Blankets and Scarves.......................... 30

Blunt Edge in Garment Construction...........................31

Reverse Hem Variations.. 34

Blunt Edge Finish Embellishments 40

    Blunt Edge Appliqué Methods......................... 40

    Double-Sided Appliqué Methods..................... 43

    Reverse Appliqué 45

Fleece Yarn 48

    Laced Edge 49

    Knitted Fleece... 50

Blunt Edge Idea Gallery 52

    Horse Motif Blanket or Throw 52

    Horse Appliqué Pillow/Multiple Pillow Sizes..... 53

    Reversible Vest..55

    Reversible Shawl Collar Jacket........................ 56

    Coordinate Crusher Hat 59

    Coordinate Scarf... 60

    Trees Jacket..61

    Snowflake Reverse Appliqué Scarf.................. 62

Chapter 4: Cheater's Wrapped Edge Finish 63

Wrapped Edge – The Cheater's Way........................64

Trim Choices...66

Finished Width Guidelines 67

Splicing Trim 69

More Ideas for Cheater's Wrapped Edge..................70

Chapter 5: Chenille.. 72

Fleece Chenille Basics...73

Chenille Yardage..76

Chenille Strips...76

Chenille Idea Gallery...78

    Jaguar Jacket..78

    Basket Weave Scarf 80

    Diamond Chenille Scarf..................................82

    Chenille Robe 83

    Coordinate Chenille Tote 85

    Chenille Appliqué...87

More Ideas for Chenille...89

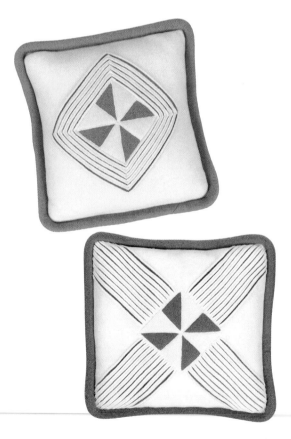

Chapter 6: Quick Fringe.....................................**91**

Quick Fringe Basics...92

Quick Fringe Technique 93

Quick Fringe Idea Gallery.......................................94

    Single-Layer Scarf...94

    Double-Layer Scarf..95

    Single-Layer Blanket – Quick Fringed on Two Sides...........96

    Single-Layer Blanket – Quick Fringed on Four Sides.........97

    Double-Layer Blanket – Quick Fringed on Two Sides.......98

    Double-Layer Blanket – Quick Fringed on Four Sides......99

    No-Sew Blanket...100

    No-Sew Pillow...102

    Simple Rag Quilt...103

    Bunny Ears Baby Blanket 105

    Boa...107

    Curly Boa..108

    Beaded Vest and Scarf...................................110

Chapter 7: Putting the Techniques to Use.................**112**

Chenille Crusher Hat and Coordinate Scarf.................113

Fleece Chenille Baby Blanket....................................116

Crystal Snowflake Scarf..120

No-Side-Seam Chenille Vest......................................121

Patchwork Embroidered Quilt...................................124

Quilted Blanket Panel...126

Quilter's Pillow..128

Scalloped Fleece Yarn...130

Ombre Embroidered Scarf...132

Stitch Effects Scarf...133

Sunshine Blanket...134

Southwest Throw..136

Southwest Pillows...137

Kokopelli Throw..140

Kokopelli Pillow/Multiple Pillow Sizes.......................141

Sweet Dreams Blanket 142

**Chapter 8: Multi-Size Jacket Pattern –
      Fit Information and Construction** **144**

Pattern Fit...145

Using a Multi-Size Pattern.......................................145

Materials Needed...145

Cutting Directions...146

General Sewing Directions..146

About the Author **149**

Resources **150**

Templates **151**

Index...**158**

INTRODUCTION

The concept for this book developed in a unique manner.

As I travel around the country presenting fleece seminars to sewers and fleece lovers, I continually add new items and variations to my trunk show. It's fun to watch the reaction of the audience when I pull items from my bag of goodies. Immediately I am asked, "Is that in one of your books?"

And my answer is rather ambiguous. "Yes, the technique is in one of my books," but "Not exactly," because I have expanded on the idea and used it in a different way. I can always count on the follow-up comment, "Gee, I never would have thought of doing that."

More Polar Magic draws on many techniques featured in my previous books (plus some new ones). However, the techniques are expanded, changed, tweaked, manipulated, and used in a wide range of applications.

Although this book includes 50 projects, it offers much more than step-by-step directions. Included are many explanations and the "logic" to an embellishment or technique so that you can see how to incorporate these techniques into other areas of your everyday sewing.

And that brings me to this newest book in my "Fleece Adventures" series. My goal is to help you visualize the expanded possibilities of all sewing techniques. As you will quickly see, many embellishment techniques take on a different personality when applied to fleece. Not all results are purposely planned. Some just happen.

I hope as you read through the different techniques and projects, you enjoy them "as is." But mostly I want you use them as a springboard to go on to create your own projects.

Have fun and enjoy.

Love,

Nancy Cornwell

P.S. I am constantly asked, "What pattern did you use?" This time the answer is easy. The pattern for the Jaguar Jacket on the cover (and three variations) is included at the back of the book!

Chapter 1

Quick Refresher Course

This chapter serves as a quick refresher, highlighting the basics for successful fleece sewing. It is not intended to be an in-depth "everything-you'll-ever-need-to-know" information source for garment construction. Just a reminder of the basics.

Fleece is not a temperamental or difficult fabric. As a matter of fact, it has a very forgiving nature and is quite easy to sew on… if you know a few simple but important rules.

Nancy's Golden Rules

- Loosen Up
- Lighten Up
- Tape It Up
- If the Conditions Change, the Rules Change

It's amazing how many times the most common questions or problems are answered by one of my Golden Rules. I came up with these Golden Rules when asked for a quick synopsis of the most important things to keep in mind at all times. So…

● LOOSEN UP

I should really say "lengthen up" but in this day and age the term "loosen up" is easier to remember. And it fits right in with the comfortable, easy nature of fleece. While I am all for sipping a glass of chilled white wine during evening sewing sessions (white wine because it doesn't stain if you happen to spill), I am by no means encouraging sewers to be "loose women." I am reminding you to lengthen the stitch length on both your conventional sewing machine and serger when sewing on fleece. Lengthen the stitch to a minimum of 3mm. I cannot stress enough the importance of this simple stitch length adjustment.

Remember Ruffled Rib

If you consider the logic behind sewing with longer stitches, you will never again forget to loosen up.

The logic: Remember how to make ruffled rib trim – that feminine, frilly, lettuce-edged finish on ribbing collars and cuffs? To get the rippled effect, you hold the folded edge of the ribbing between both hands, pull the ribbing taut, and zigzag stitch over the edge using a wide, dense satin stitch. In reality, you are sewing incorrectly for a purpose.

You stretch the ribbing and cover the edge with stitches so when you let go of the stretched ribbing, it cannot bounce back to its original dimension because there is too much thread piled in. The result is a distorted, wavy edge. On ribbing, it ruffles and looks pretty. On fleece garments, it manifests itself in wavy hems, buckled zippers, and frog-mouth buttonholes.

Ribbing is a stretch fabric. So is fleece. The same thing happens if you use a too-short stitch length when sewing hems, seams, zippers, pockets, or buttonholes. If you force in too many stitches or too much thread,

the fleece will stretch and wave. Pretty when making ruffled rib… not pretty in garment construction!

Nancy's Hint

Because this is a fleece book, I address stitch length as it relates to fleece. However, you can apply this logic to all your stretch knit sewing. The results are the same whether you are sewing on interlock, sweatshirting, jersey, knit terry, or velour. If you are working on a stretch knit, lengthen your stitch length.

This means you don't just turn on your machine and sew. Most newer sewing machines have a default stitch length setting of 2.25mm to 2.5mm, which is approximately 12 to 14 stitches per inch. This is based on the assumption that you are sewing on a traditional woven fabric. This shorter stitch length is appropriate for woven fabrics but it is not appropriate for knit fabrics. (Remember ruffled rib.)

When sewing with fleece, adjust your stitch length to at least 3mm, or approximately nine stitches per inch. I usually stitch at 3.5mm (approximately seven stitches per inch). And when stitching bulky multiple layers, sewing on the crossgrain (with the stretch) or inserting zippers, I increase the stitch length to 4mm.

Nancy's Note

This longer stitch length is appropriate for casual fleece garments with no high-stress seams. If sewing a tight-fitting Lycra blend fleece garment with high-stress seams, use "Lycra rules" rather than "fleece rules." Shorten the stitch length to 12 to 14 stitches per inch. In the relaxed state, the seams may ripple, but when stretched on the body they will be smooth and strong.

Recap

If your seam waves…

If your zipper buckles…

If your buttonhole "frog mouths"…

If your pockets bubble…

If your fleece balks at feeding under the presser foot…

Lengthen the stitch length.

(If you only remember one rule, this is the one.)

For detailed information covering all the important principles and techniques for successful sewing on fleece, refer to my first book, *Adventures With Polarfleece®*. It covers all the nuts-and-bolts, meat-and-potatoes information for sewing with fleece. I am proud this book won Primedia's Best Sewing Book of 1998 Award.

● LIGHTEN UP

Fleece is bulkier than most fabrics in your sewing stash. If you find your fleece balking at feeding through the machine, first try the Loosen Up approach (lengthen your stitch length). This makes the feed teeth move in larger increments, grab the fabric in bigger bites, and help feed the fabric through under the presser foot.

Most of the time, lengthening the stitch length corrects the difficulty. If you have an older machine that gets a little temperamental and the longer stitch length doesn't help enough, lessen the pressure on the presser foot. This allows the fleece to feed through, and the lighter pressure, combined with the longer stitch length, reduces the tendency of fleece layers to shift alignment.

● TAPE IT UP

Always have Wash-Away Wonder Tape on hand. (I use it so much that I keep two packages on hand at all times.) This double-sided, wash-away, stitch-through basting tape is a blessing for so many applications. Don't waste time pinning when you can tape with better success.

Nancy's Note

Whenever I mention a brand name product, it is because I have personally used it and been pleased with the results. In this day and age, with new products constantly being introduced, there may be other comparable products.

There are many basting tapes or similar adhesive tapes on the market.

However, when you read the package label, they may specify "do not stitch through the tape" (it will gum up the needle) and "remove after use."

I prefer Collins Wash-Away Wonder Tape because you can stitch through it without gumming up your needle. (As you will see in the Patchwork Embroidered Quilt on page 124, the Patchwork Scarf on page 24, and the Patchwork Jacket on page 26, I stitched through this tape for yards and yards without getting a sticky needle.) And there's no need to remove it since it launders away in the first wash. (It's not my idea of fun trying to remove tape from fleece!)

Look for the words "wash away" to be sure you have the correct product.

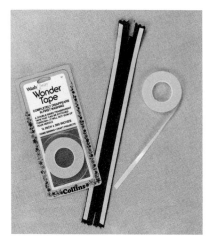

Wash-away basting tape and a longer stitch length ensure flat zippers every time. (Great for all zipper insertions, not just fleece!)

Tape zippers in place for perfect, flat zippers every time. (Read the No-Hassle Zippers chapter in *Adventures With Polarfleece*® for detailed instructions on a variety of zipper applications and treatments.) Tape instead of pin, and lengthen your stitch length.

Instead of pin-and-stitch, tape-and-stitch, use wash-away basting tape to:
• tape "baste" zippers in place
• tape pockets in place

• tape decorative trim in place
• match plaids for perfect alignment
• spot hold appliqués
• tape "baste" lapped seams

While I recommend this product for use on fleece (because this is a fleece book), I use it in all areas of my sewing.

● IF THE CONDITIONS CHANGE, THE RULES CHANGE

This rule almost seems all too obvious, yet in the everyday sequence of sewing, we rarely think about it. Its most important application is probably in connection with needle choice. When you read the information regarding needles, consider those guidelines as a starting point, subject to change as conditions dictate.

Choose the needle *size* according to the *weight* of the fabric. Choose the needle *type* according to the fabric, thread, and type of sewing you are doing.

For example, if you are sewing on mid-weight fleece using the recommended 90/14 needle, and all of a sudden you have an area where you are stitching through three or four layers of fleece (the conditions changed), replace the 90/14 needle with a larger 100/16 needle size. The medium size needle will handle the mid-weight fleece under normal conditions, but the added weight and bulk of multiple layers will

cause the needle to bend and possibly skip stitches or break.

As for needle *type*, choose a universal or ballpoint for general fleece sewing.

If you decide to apply an UltraSuede appliqué on the fleece, change to a stretch needle to accommodate the demands of UltraSuede. UltraSuede is fussier than fleece and sews nicer with a stretch needle.

If you decide to topstitch with metallic thread on the UltraSuede appliqué on the fleece, choose a needle type to accommodate metallic thread (because metallic thread is fussier than UltraSuede, which is fussier than fleece). In this instance, you should choose the needle type according to the metallic thread demands – generally a 90/14 metallic, embroidery, or topstitch needle.

Choose the needle type according to the "fussiest" element of your sewing.

Fabric Basics

Polyester fleece comes in a wide range of colors, prints, textures, qualities, and prices. Fleece can be produced domestically or imported from the Orient. The quality will vary from trademarked brands to generic brands.

The most recognized trademarked names (also the highest quality) are Polarfleece and Polartec from Malden Mills (U.S.), Nordic Fleece from David Textiles, Inc. (imported), Solar Fleece from Siltex Mills (Canada), and Yukon Fleece from Huntingdon Mills (Canada).

Fabric and Garment Care

Pretreating

There's no need to pretreat the fabric since fleece does not shrink or shed excess color. You can buy it and sew immediately!

Laundering

To avoid unnecessary abrasion, wash finished garments inside out and with similar garments. Use a powdered detergent, lukewarm water, and the gentle cycle. Don't use bleach or any type of softening agent (liquid or dryer sheets). Toss in the dryer on low heat for a short time.

Most of the fleeces found in fabric stores and featured throughout this book are fun, fashion fleeces. If you prefer to use liquid detergent, it will not harm them. However, if you purchase high-tech fleece, with technical finishes designed to protect against severe weather elements, definitely use a powdered detergent. Don't risk losing those protective features you paid extra money to have.

Avoid softening agents in both the washer and the dryer. Softeners are lubricants and will soften the hand of fleece, making it limp.

Nancy's Note

Powdered detergent is recommended by the manufacturers to protect any chemical finishes that may have been applied to the fleece. Liquid detergent and/or softeners may negate any water repellant, anti-microbial, or other technical finishes applied to performance fleece.

Drying

Fleece is hydrophobic, meaning it doesn't like water. With its polyester fiber content and construction, fleece naturally resists retaining water. When you remove a fleece garment from the washer, it feels damp, not soaking wet. You can shake and hang it to dry. If you want to tumble it in the dryer to relax wrinkles and speed up the drying process, turn it inside out and dry it on gentle/low heat for 10 minutes or so.

Nancy's Disclaimer

I stated earlier that fleece doesn't shrink. However, any polyester fabric tossed in the dryer on high heat will end up with tightened yarns, which causes shrinkage.

Nancy's Note

I am careful not to dry fleece with garments or fabrics that shed a lot of lint (garments that leave a layer of lint in the lint trap). The polyester nap of fleece tends to grab onto and hold lint (like when a facial tissue inadvertently sneaks into the dryer).

Pressing

Not recommended. If, during the construction stage, you feel a compelling urge to press, hold the iron above the fleece and steam it. Then gently finger press to encourage the fleece to lay in the desired position. Never place an iron soleplate in direct contact with fleece. Direct contact may leave a permanent iron imprint on the fleece.

Nancy's Disclaimer

There are times in my More Polarfleece® Adventures and Polar Magic books when I instruct you to iron a stabilizer onto the wrong side of the fleece to do a specific embellishment technique. Iron with a dry iron and a light touch. The iron should never come in direct contact with the fleece, but touch only the stabilizer.

On page 133 you will see that it is possible to press iron-on transfers onto fleece. The small soleplate of the Clover Mini Iron allows you to successfully do certain heat embellishment applications without damaging the nap.

Which is the Right Side?

To find the right side of fleece, stretch it along the cut edge on the crossgrain (direction of most stretch). The fleece will curl to the *wrong* side.

Remember this. You'll use it often.

Always test for the right side of the fabric.

Nancy's Important Note

*Many times throughout this book you will handle a small piece of fleece (a square, a patch, or an appliqué). To determine the right side of the fabric, gently pull on the cut edges in all directions of the piece. Fleece has decidedly more stretch on the crossgrain. After determining the cut edge with the most stretch, tug along that cut edge and the fleece will curl to the **wrong** side.*

General Sewing Basics

Sewing Machine, Serger, and Embroidery Machine

Make sure your machines are cleaned, oiled, and in good working order. Sewing with fleece results in a lot of lint. Clean your machines frequently.

Thread

Choose good quality, long staple polyester thread that matches your fleece color or is a shade darker. Don't be tempted by bargain threads that will easily fray and break.

Nancy's Hint

Since threads sink into the loft of fleece, color match is not critical. If I don't have a good match on hand, I choose something that blends easily — black or navy on dark-colored fleece, medium gray on mid-tones, white or cream on pastels.

Needles

Always begin a project with a fresh, new needle.

Because fleece is a knitted fabric, choose a universal, stretch, or ballpoint needle. These needles have rounded points that deflect rather than pierce the yarn.

Choose the needle *size* according to the *weight* of the fleece. Use the smallest size possible that is strong enough to do the job.

Nancy's Hint

If you experience skipped stitches or break a needle, go up one needle size. If you are using an older temperamental machine and experiencing skipped stitches, try using a zigzag stitch 3mm to 4mm long and .5mm to 1mm wide.

Choose the needle *type* according to the fabric type, thread choice, and type of sewing you are doing. Choose the needle type according to the fussiest element of your sewing.

Nancy's Reminder

If the conditions change, the rules change. It never fails to amaze me how many machine problems are corrected by a simple needle change.

For in-depth fleece fabric information and fleece construction techniques, please refer to the book *Adventures With Polarfleece®*.

Yardage

Fleece comes 60" wide, so all yardage requirements are based on that width.

Handy Guess-timate Chart

It never fails. You are in your favorite sewing shop, buying totally unrelated products when you spy a drop-dead, gotta-have, gorgeous fleece print. You don't have a clue what pattern you are going to use, but you just have to have it.

Make a copy of this handy little guide and keep it in your wallet. Use these yardages as a basic guideline for how much to buy.

Safety Tip

If you are buying a print with a pattern repeat, it's advisable to estimate your yardage, then add one extra repeat for insurance. (This extra yardage gives you the versatility to arrange and rearrange pieces to best complement the pattern print on your garment without worrying about fabric shortage.)

NEEDLE SIZE GUIDELINES

Lightweight fleece	Mid-weight fleece	Heavyweight fleece
size 70/10 or 75/11	size 80/12 or 90/14	size 100/16

NEEDLE TYPE GUIDELINES

Regular construction sewing	Rayon thread	Metallic thread
universal, ballpoint, or stretch needle	embroidery needle	metallic, topstitch, or embroidery needle, size 90/14 or larger

NANCY'S QUICK REFERENCE YARDAGE GUESS-TIMATE GUIDE FOR 60" FLEECE

Simple pullover or jacket with polar ribbing finish
1¾ to 2 yards (add ½ yard for hood)

Simple pullover or jacket from a double-border print
2 to 2¼ yards (add ½ yard for hood)

Simple vest
¾ to 1 yard

Simple vest, double-border print
¾ to 1 yard

Scarf
¼ to ⅓ yard

Throw
1½ yards

Blanket
2 yards

Baby blanket
1¼ yards

Pillow
5" more than pillow form size

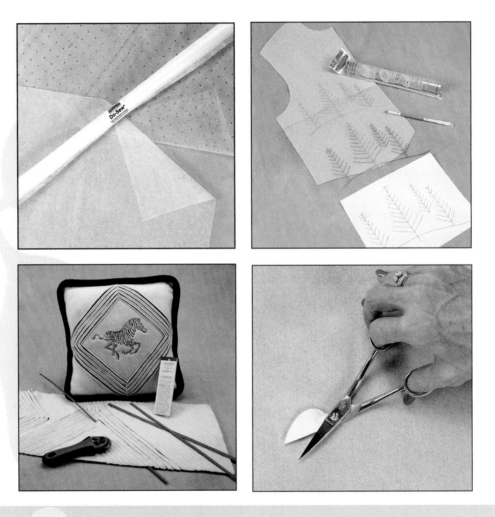

Chapter 2

Gotta-Have Notions

(Also known as "sewing assistants")
One day as I was leafing through a Nancy's Notions catalog,
I came across Nancy Zieman's term for notions — "sewing assistants."
I loved it. That's exactly what these tools are.

New "sewing assistants" come into the marketplace almost daily. That means I have additions to the "gotta-have" notions lists from my earlier books. Many of the notions and tools listed here are old standby favorites used in a different way.

Whenever brand name products are mentioned, it is because I have personally used them and been pleased with the results. There may be other comparable products.

References

Adventures With Polarfleece®

This is an obviously biased opinion, but I am proud of this book. It has become acknowledged as the sewing industry's "polar encyclopedia." This is the resource handbook for in-depth fleece information, sewing machine and serger techniques, what to look for in patterns, seam options, ready-to-wear edge finishes, no-hassle zipper applications (from practical to designer applications), buttonholes (standard, fashion, and troubleshooting), UltraSuede accents, plus an introduction to sculpturing and texturing fleece. Included are projects to sew. If you are new to sewing fleece, this book is a must for your sewing library.

More Polarfleece® Adventures

Another obviously biased opinion. While I am proud of the first book, I had a ball writing the second book. Answering the demand for more embellishment techniques, this book picks up where the first book left off. Creating textures and surface interest using a conventional sewing machine. Pure and simple playing, this book expands on the concept of sculpturing, including double-needle sculpturing and decorative stitch sculpturing. It teaches pintucking for dimension, "to-die-for" polar ribbing, cutwork and appliqué, more buttonholes, and edge finishes.

Polar Magic

This award-winning book taps into today's most popular sewing areas – fleece, quilting, machine embroidery, and home dec. *Polar Magic* encourages "cross-over sewing" by incorporating traditionally nonfleece techniques into everyday fleece sewing. Trapunto, chenille, embossing, pintucking, machine embroidery, and reverse appliqué techniques are applied to fleece with dramatic results. The large chapter on fleece home dec is loaded with creative ideas for all ages.

Embroidery Machine Essentials: Fleece Techniques

This book combines the excitement of machine embroidery with the popularity of fleece.

After learning a variety of methods for embroidering on fleece and using embroidery for subtle surface interest, you'll learn how to look for and extract "hidden designs" from each motif. Apply this approach to your embroidery library and each design's potential grows exponentially! The book includes a CD with 20 exclusive original designs.

Notions

Wash-Away Wonder Tape

I have recommended this double-sided basting tape in all my books. I choose this basting tape because the ¼" width has terrific holding power, you can sew through it without gumming up the needle, and because it doesn't need to be removed – it launders away! Look for the words "wash-away" to be sure you have the correct product.

Wonder Tape is perfect for holding garment pieces in place where pins would be awkward. Because it prevents shifting of layers, it is the *only* way to "baste" zippers and pockets in place. It is also very convenient to spot hold appliqué and decorative trims.

Long Glass Head or Flower Head Pins

Pins can easily get buried or lost in the loft of fleece. For best visibility (thus avoiding unwanted contact with serger blades), choose longer pins. When pinning, place the pins at a 90° angle to the seamline or cut edges.

Water-Soluble Pencils

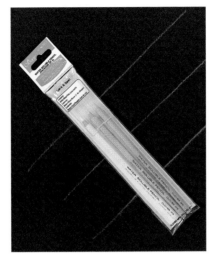

In my earlier books I extolled the virtues of Clover's Chacopel pencils. I still love them, but now they offer a water-soluble version I love even more! The Clover water-soluble pencils are fabric marking pencils that mark easily on fleece and *stay marked* until erased with water. I find other marking tools are either too difficult to see or they rub off too easily when handling the fabric.

Caution: Sharpen these pencils to a medium point. An over-sharpened point breaks too easily.

Nancy's Hint

Instead of going to the sink and dabbing with a wet cloth or tossing in the washer to erase water-soluble markings, here's a quick way to remove markings right in your sewing room. Go to an office supply store and get one of those sponge-tipped envelope moistener pen-shaped tools and keep it with your sewing tools. Squeeze to wet the sponge and easily dab the marks away.

Mesh Transfer Canvas

This handy notion from Clover makes transferring designs and motifs onto fleece a very simple process. Mesh transfer canvas is a 12" x 16" piece of fine gauge plastic mesh. It has the benefit of being reusable over and over again. Use a Chacopel or regular pencil if you want to reuse the canvas. Use a permanent pen if you want it to serve as a permanent template.

Simply lay the mesh canvas over the motif and trace with a Chacopel pencil. Then lay the traced mesh canvas on your fleece and redraw the design again with a Chacopel pencil. The pencil marks go through the little mesh holes, easily transferring the design onto the fleece. Quick and easy!

Need to reverse the design? Simply flip the traced mesh canvas over. There's no need to use a light box or sunny window to reverse motifs.

Nancy's Hint

Mesh transfer canvas has found a welcome place in many areas around the house. It's great for school projects, woodworking, and needle arts. Any time you need to get a design from one place to another, use mesh transfer canvas. Simply wash it with soap and water and it's ready for the next use.

Sulky's KK2000 Temporary Adhesive Spray

This innovative product is the solution to many "holding" predicaments. It is used extensively throughout my books to make a wide variety of applications and techniques much easier. The beauty of this spray adhesive is that it absorbs into the fibers in two or three days and completely disappears in three to 10 days. (The timing depends on the amount sprayed, fabric type, heat, humidity conditions, and air circulation.) The simple explanation: the molecular structure breaks down, prohibiting the chemicals, glues, and propellants from hardening. There will be absolutely no residue remaining on the fabric.

The heavier-than-air propellant is not petroleum based, so it is not flammable. Because the spray is heavy, you can hold the can as close as 6" to 10" from your fabric. It goes exactly where you want it without wasteful overspray.

Important KK2000 Caution #1: Spray KK2000 on the surface that will be removed rather than on the fleece itself. For example, lightly spray KK2000 adhesive on the stabilizer and then adhere it to the fleece. When you remove the stabilizer, most of the adhesive will be removed with it, leaving only a trace amount on the fleece (which disappears over time). Spray the KK2000 on an appliqué and adhere it to the fleece. This keeps the appliqué exactly where you want it with no room for error.

Important Caution #2: Spray lightly. KK2000 has terrific holding power and does not need to be heavily applied. Excessive adhesive takes much longer to disappear.

Important Caution #3: KK2000 is not water-soluble. It doesn't wash out or rinse away. Any contact with water results in a gummy residue that is difficult to remove. It is formulated to dissolve on its own – don't interfere with the process.

Important Caution #4: Machine manufacturers recommend that when applying any spray adhesive, you work in an area totally removed from your conventional sewing machine, serger, and embroidery machine. This precautionary step ensures that no adhesive comes in contact with the tension discs or any other sensitive machine mechanism. Better safe than sorry!

Nancy's Comment

The two most important reasons I use this product are the terrific holding power I get from using minimal spray and the control I have over the spray, without overspray.

Nancy's Hint

If you ever find a gummy residue on your fleece (from inadvertent water contact on the adhesive or heavy overspraying), rubbing alcohol does a nice job of removing the unwanted residue.

Omnistrips Cutting Mats

These are long, skinny, mini cutting mats from Omnigrid, Inc. designed for precision cutting in tiny places. They are perfect for making fleece faux chenille. The strips come in a variety of sizes from ¼" to ⅝". I most often use the ¼", ⁵⁄₁₆", and ⅜" mini strips when making fleece chenille.

Rotary Cutters

Rotary cutters are available from several companies. While the standard 45mm blade size works just fine, I prefer to use the larger 60mm size. The larger blade effortlessly handles the fleece bulk and the corresponding larger handle is comfortable to use, making it easier on my hands. (I now use the larger blade for all my cutting needs.)

Choose the medium 45mm rotary decorative blades (wave, pinking, scallop) for specialty edge finishes.

I particularly like to use the wave and the scallop blade for a decorative blunt edge finish. The edge finish is easy and attractive.

Olfa offers a variety of specialty blades. The wave blade gives a soft, gentle fleece edge. The pinking blade finish lends a crafty flavor. The Olfa scallop blade offers a dual benefit: Depending on how you attach the blade and/or cut the fabric, you can have either a scallop or peaked edge. (*Always* do a sample test cut when using the scallop blade to make sure you are getting the edge shape you want.)

Nancy's Note
There are many decorative blade scissors on the market that are designed for use on paper and perhaps flat cotton. They do not work well on fleece.

Appliqué Scissors

With the flat, disc-shaped, underside blade, appliqué scissors provide close, accurate trimming on a top layer of fabric while protecting the remaining under layer of fabric from unintentional nicks and cuts. They are the best way to achieve a clean blunt edge trim on all appliqués. They are a "must-have" notion in your sewing room.

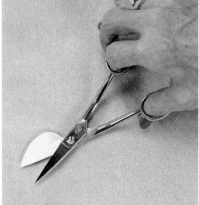

Electric Scissors from Dritz

One swipe with these scissors and I was in love!

Fleece chenille is easy to make, but the multiple channels can be tedious to cut and hard on the hands. The electric scissors slice through the fleece like a hot knife through butter. Quick. Easy. Accurate. Comfortable (the vibration of the scissor is almost like a mini hand massage).

Electric scissors broaden chenille design possibilities by offering the opportunity to stitch wavy and curved channels. (While I love Omnistrips, they do limit me to straight line stitching channels.) I still need the channels to be sewn predominantly on the bias, but now I can change directions, curl, and swirl because the electric scissors can go almost anywhere.

I love electric scissors for general cutting of cottons and other woven fabrics. However, when it comes to cutting out fleece garments, I still prefer my rotary cutter. (The electric scissors are not recommended for material over ⅛" thick due to the short cutting stroke.)

Mini Iron from Clover

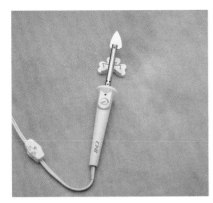

This is one of those obvious, "Why didn't I think of that?" inventions that you will use over and over. It's a great little tool to have alongside your sewing machine for pressing seams open, whether quilting or tailoring. No more running back and forth to the ironing board!

Aside from all the practical quilting and construction uses, I love the Mini Iron because it gives me a way to apply heat-activated embellishments to fleece. The small soleplate makes it easy to press trims and appliqués onto fleece without the risk of flattening the fleece nap, something you can't avoid with the large soleplate of a traditional iron.

The Mini Iron has multiple temperature settings, making it versatile for many applications.

Stiletto

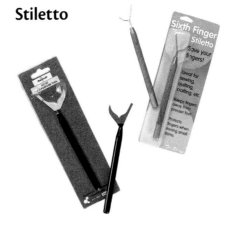

This is another example of "borrowing" tools from different sewing arenas and using them with fleece. The stiletto is a well-known tool used to tame ribbon in silk ribbon embroidery and to help feed fabric into binders for edge finishes. However, this simple little tool is overlooked (and underappreciated) for its tremendous versatility.

When sewing fleece, I find myself reaching for it constantly. The thin, flat prong allows me to get close to the needle without impairing visibility. The pointed prong gives just the right nudge when a fabric doesn't want to cooperate. Whether stitching a blunt edge appliqué, attaching trim, applying elastic or ribbing, feeding bulky layers of fleece under the presser foot, or keeping a topping in place, I find the stiletto to be in constant use.

Pattern Tracing Material

I always use pattern tracing material to trace individual sizes and variations when using a multi-size pattern (like the jacket pattern included at the back of this book). This allows me to preserve the master pattern for future use and reuse. I prefer pattern tracing "material" rather than "paper" because it doesn't tear and can be ironed if wrinkled. Use a soft lead pencil to trace. Don't use ballpoint or ink that could possibly transfer onto your fashion fabric.

Do-Sew from Stretch & Sew, Inc., dotted pattern tracing cloth from Staple Sewing Aids Corp., and Pellon Quilter's Grid can be found at your favorite fabric store.

Chapter 3

Blunt Edge Finish

The blunt edge finish (also called raw edge) is a simple technique that offers so many practical and embellishment applications that its uses keep growing. Team the nonravel characteristic with the lofty nature of fleece and you have the perfect conditions for using the cut raw edge of the fleece "as is."

Single-Layer – Lapped Seams and Patchwork

Blunt edge finish techniques are very practical for blankets and scarves. Use either a straight or specialty rotary blade, depending on the look you want.

When you cut fleece fabric, if the cut edge is crisp, clean, and blunt, you can use that cut edge to your advantage to avoid bulk and to make many otherwise tedious techniques quick and simple.

Quick fringe, chenille, and cheater's wrapped edge are all forms of the blunt edge finish. However, they are each so versatile that they warrant their own chapters.

Patchwork Embroidered Quilt

The wave blade rotary cutter and wash-away basting tape made this quilt a breeze to put together. The wrong side of the quilt looks just as good as the right side!

Cutting the squares with the wave blade (for a pretty edge finish), then taping instead of pinning the squares together, are the secrets to making this quilt.

Step-by-step directions can be found on page 124.

Patchwork Scarf

This pretty decorative-edged scarf is one of those projects that looks more difficult than it is. Fleece's nonravel characteristic, teamed with lapped seam construction, a decorative scallop rotary blade, and wash-away basting tape, make this scarf quick and easy to sew. (Hmm. Does this give you an idea for a different way to approach crazy patch projects?)

MATERIALS

Fleece color #1 (pink): ¼ yard

Fleece color #2 (blue): ¼ yard

Fleece color #3 (white): ¼ yard

Wash-away basting tape

Scallop rotary blade

Thread to blend with all

DIRECTIONS

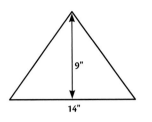

1. Draw a triangle pattern piece 14" wide at the base and 9" high.

2. Cut four pink triangles, three blue triangles, and three white triangles.

3. Place all the triangles right side up on a table. (Pull gently in the direction of the most stretch. The fleece will curl toward the *wrong* side.)

4. Build the patchwork scarf from left to right, with the left patch always overlapping the patch on its right.

a. Place a strip of basting tape on the left edge of the blue triangle.

b. Overlap a pink triangle on the blue triangle by ½" and adhere.

c. Stitch the layers together using a wavy or serpentine stitch to complement the scalloped edge. Align the right edge of the presser foot to the top of the rounded scallop. (It's always best to test stitch on a scrap first.)

d. Place basting tape on the left edge of a white triangle.

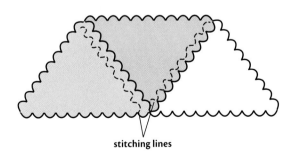

stitching lines

e. Overlap the pink/blue segment on the white triangle and adhere.

f. Stitch the layers together.

g. Continue building the scarf, ending with a pink triangle.

Nancy's Notes

Choose a simple, waved straight stitch. Avoid satin stitches or multi-motion (back-and-forth) stitches, as they build too much thread into the seam and distort the fleece. Test the stitches on a scrap first, adjusting the length and width until you have one you like.

Since the stitches sink into the loft of the fleece, thread color match is not critical. I used white in both the needle and the bobbin. It blended in beautifully!

Patchwork Jacket

This is a fun variation of the jacket pattern included with this book. I thought this would be a great opportunity to do a little redesigning of the basic jacket pattern. If you have another patchwork idea in mind, use this same approach and draw your own design lines.

This jacket takes advantage of the fleece raw edge to build the patchwork front. Cut the designated patch section with a decorative scallop blade, overlap and tape it to a neighboring patch, and stitch in place.

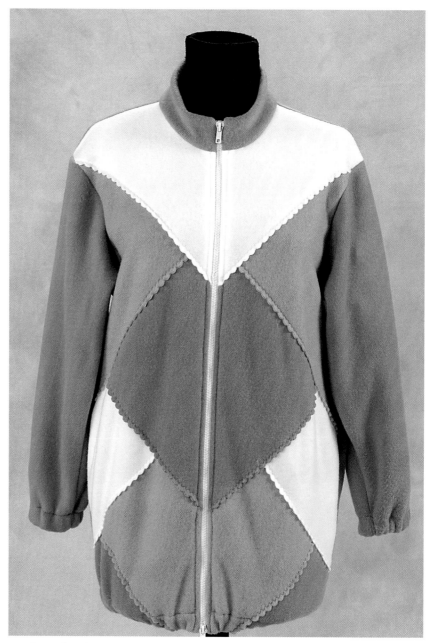

Tape, lap, and stitch sections together, building patchwork from the bottom up.

MATERIALS

Fleece main color (blue): 1¾ yards

Fleece contrast color #1 (pink): ⅝ yard

Fleece contrast color #2 (white): ½ yard

Jacket pattern in back of book

Decorative scallop rotary blade

Pattern tracing material

Wash-away basting tape

Separating zipper (see page 145)

Nancy's Note

Using this technique, you only need to allow a seam allowance on the overlapping scalloped edge. If you were redesigning a patchwork front and wanted to sew the patches together in the traditional manner (rather than overlapping), you would need to add seam allowances to all the patchwork edges that would be stitched into seams.

DIRECTIONS

Draft the Pattern Front

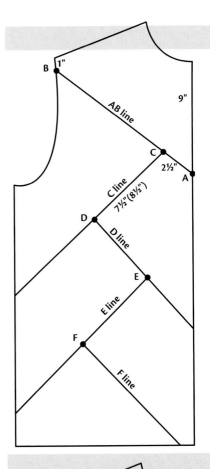

1. Using pattern tracing material, trace one jacket front from the multi-size pattern included in the back of the book. Trace for the elastic lower edge finish.

2. Mark dot A on the center front edge, 9" below the neck edge.

3. Mark dot B on the armscye edge, 1" below the shoulder edge.

4. Draw the AB line.

5. Mark dot C on the AB line, 2½" from the center front edge.

6. Draw the C line perpendicular to the AB line, from dot C to the side seam edge.

7. Mark dot D on the C line, 7½" from dot C (for small and medium) or 8½" from dot C (for large and x-large).

8. Draw the D line perpendicular to the C line, from dot D to the center front edge.

9. Mark dot E on the D line, halfway between dot D and the center front edge.

10. Draw the E line perpendicular to the D line, from dot E to the side seam edge.

11. Mark dot F on the E line, halfway between dot E and the side seam edge.

12. Draw the F line perpendicular to the E line, from dot F to the lower edge.

MARK THE PATCHWORK SECTIONS

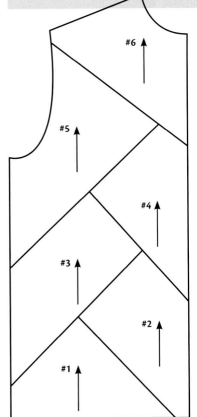

◀ 1. Draw a straight-of-grain line in each patch, drawing an arrow at the top of the grainline to designate the top edge of the patchwork piece. (This will be helpful during construction.) Number each patch as shown.

▶ 2. Before cutting the patchwork front pattern piece apart, carefully mark the edges to be cut with a decorative scallop blade and the seam allowances to be added to patches #2, #3, #4, #5, and #6. (There is no scallop edge on patch #1.)

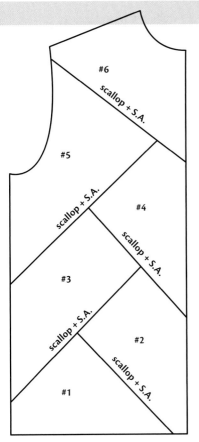

Cut the Pieces

Nancy's Hint

To add a ³⁄₈" seam allowance with a scallop edge, lay a ruler ¼" away from the original line and cut with a scallop blade.

1. Using the multi-size jacket pattern included at the back of the book, cut the following:

- From main fleece color (blue)
  - 1 back (on fold) elastic finish
  - 2 sleeves (elastic finish)
  - 1 collar (plain)
  - 2 #1 patches (cut lower edge with scallop blade, adding ³⁄₈" seam allowance)
  - 2 #4 patches (cut lower edge with scallop blade, adding ³⁄₈" seam allowance)

- From contrast color #1 (pink)
  - 2 #2 patches (cut lower edge with scallop blade, adding ³⁄₈" seam allowance)
  - 2 #5 patches (cut lower edge with scallop blade, adding ³⁄₈" seam allowance)

- From contrast color #2 (white)
  - 2 #3 patches (cut lower edge with scallop blade, adding ³⁄₈" seam allowance)
  - 2 #6 patches (cut lower edge with scallop blade, adding ³⁄₈" seam allowance)

Construct the Jacket

Note: *For clarity, the stitching lines are not shown on the illustrations.*

Nancy's Important Notes

- *Do all construction of the jacket front with the fabric right side up.*
- *Place all wash-away basting tape on the right side of the fabric patches.*
- *Overlap the patches ³⁄₈".*
- *When stitching overlapped patches, choose a simple waved or straight stitch and adjust it to complement the decorative cut edge.*

Note: While a scallop stitch would nicely mimic the cut edge, it would be difficult to consistently match the scallop cuts.

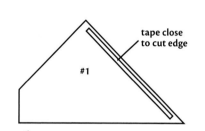

1. Place basting tape on the upper edge of patch #1.

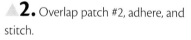

2. Overlap patch #2, adhere, and stitch.

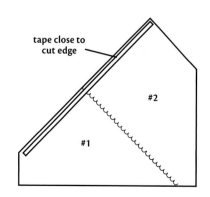

3. Place basting tape on the upper edges of patches #1 and #2.

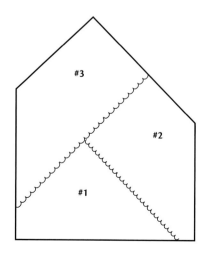

4. Overlap patch #3 onto patches #1 and #2, adhere, and stitch.

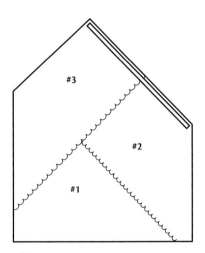

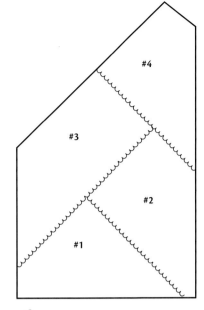

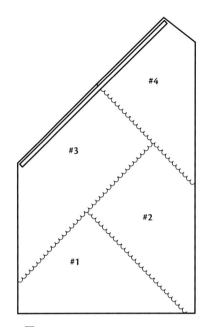

▲**5.** Place basting tape on the upper edges of patches #3 and #2.

▲**6.** Overlap patch #4 onto patches #3 and #2, adhere, and stitch.

▲**7.** Place basting tape on the upper edges of patches #3 and #4.

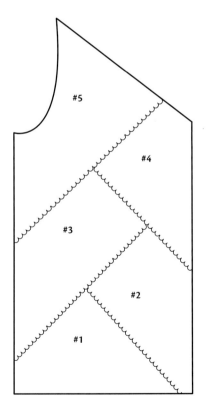

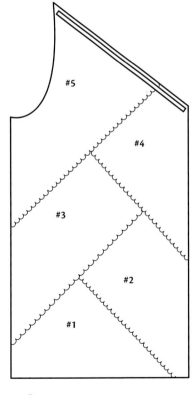

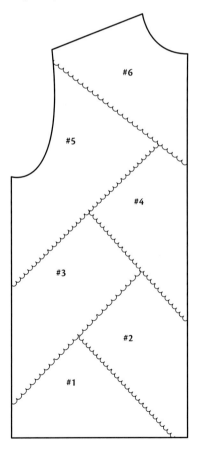

▲**8.** Overlap patch #5 onto patches #3 and #4, adhere, and stitch.

▲**9.** Place basting tape on patches #5 and #4.

▲**10.** Overlap patch #6 onto patches #5 and #4, adhere, and stitch.

11. Repeat the above steps to build the remaining patchwork front.

12. Refer to the directions on page 146 to complete the jacket construction.

Double-Layer – Blankets and Scarves

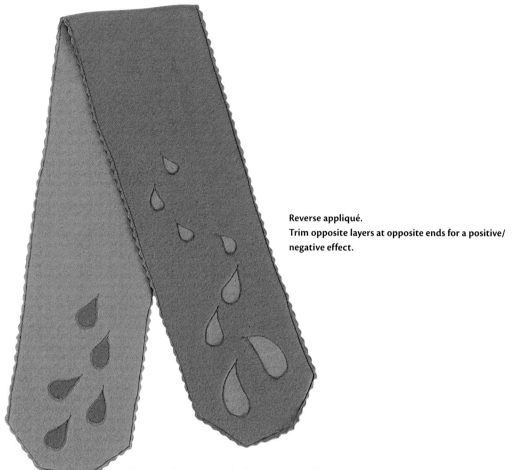

Reverse appliqué.
**Trim opposite layers at opposite ends for a positive/
negative effect.**

When dealing with a double-layer item like a blanket or scarf, the blunt edge finish is a blessing. It would be awkward and bulky to sew the two layers together using the traditional method.

Traditional Method (Awkward and Bulky)

1. Place the fabric layers right sides together.

2. Sew around the entire outer edge, leaving an opening for turning.

3. Trim the seam.

4. Turn right side out.

5. Stitch the opening closed.

Blunt Edge Method (Easy and Nonbulky)

1. Place the fabric layers *wrong* sides together (finished position).

2. Sew around the entire outer edge, using a ½" seam allowance.

3. Rotary trim close to the stitching line.

Blunt Edge Finish in Garment Construction

This cute outfit was featured in *More Polarfleece® Adventures* to demonstrate an effective use of the wave blade rotary cutter. Here it serves as a perfect example of how to incorporate a variety of blunt edge techniques into your everyday sewing.

Pockets

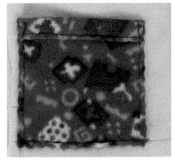

I introduced the blunt edge concept in my first book, *Adventures With Polarfleece®* as a practical and clever way to sew fleece patch pockets on a garment.

To attach a pocket, simply apply wash-away basting tape to the wrong side of the pocket edges, tape the pocket in place, edgestitch, and topstitch. Quick. Easy. Symmetrical corners every time.

Since I was playing with the decorative effects of the wave blade, I decided to make the pocket facing pretty as well as functional. I folded the top facing to the right side of the pocket (reverse hem, page 34), taped, and topstitched it in place. Then I basting taped the pocket in place and stitched it to secure.

Collars or Cuffs

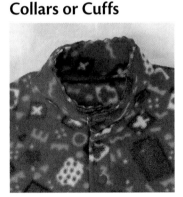

This method works for a stand-up collar, regular fold-down collar, or cuffs.

Place the collars together in the finished position (wrong sides together). Use a conventional sewing machine to stitch the collar seam outer edge. Use a rotary cutter to trim the exposed seam allowances close to the stitching line. Because this outfit is for a child, I used the wave blade to make it fun. I would use a straight blade for a more traditional appearance.

Yoke Lapped Seams

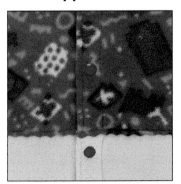

Lapped seams are easy and offer a great way to reduce bulk. The yoke shown demonstrates the effectiveness of using lapped seams when attaching a yoke to the lower garment.

1. Trim away the seam allowance from the overlapping layer.

2. Place wash-away basting tape on the *wrong* side of the yoke, close to the trimmed edge.

3. Align the yoke trimmed edge with the seamline on the body piece. Adhere.

4. If cutting with a straight blade, edgestitch, then topstitch ¼" away to secure the seam. If cutting with a decorative blade, topstitch at ¼".

Nancy's Notes

*When stitching straight-cut lapped fleece seams, **always** edgestitch, then topstitch ¼" away. The edgestitching keeps the cut edge flat but is not secure enough on its own. The additional topstitching ¼" away from the edgestitching both secures the seam and adds nice detail.*

*When designing the Patchwork Jacket front, I **added** the seam allowance to the overlapping edge. In the child's yoke lapped seam, I **removed** the seam allowance from the overlapping edge. You can go either way as long as one of the edge's seam allowances is removed. Just be consistent within the garment. I removed the seam allowance from the child's yoke to maintain visual balance on the pint-size garment.*

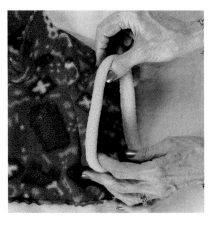

Armholes

This really belongs in the fat piping section of Chapter 4, Cheater's Wrapped Edge Finish, but since the wrapped edge is another way to take advantage of fleece's nonravel feature, I slipped it in here, too. Refer to page 68 for fat piping directions.

Embellishment

The fleece rickrack embellishment on the vest is a ⅜" strip of fleece cut with the wave blade. Place wash-away basting tape on the wrong side of the trim and adhere it in place. Attach it to the garment by straight stitching down the center of the rickrack fleece. (The basting tape won't gum up the needle.)

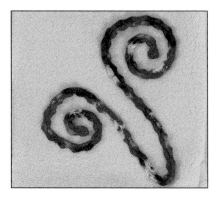

Pants Piping

For piping down the outside leg seam, cut a piece of fleece the width of the seam allowance plus a skimpy ¼" (just wide enough to peek out from the leg seam). Sandwich the piping strip between the front and back leg and incorporate it into the seam when stitching.

Mittens

These mittens aren't high-tech by any stretch of the imagination. But they're fun. Draw around a child's hand and add a little extra for wiggle room and the seam allowance. Sew with wrong sides together (finished position) and trim the exposed seam allowance with a rotary cutter. Choose ribbing scraps from your "spare ribs" stash to make the ribbing cuffs.

No bulky piping when using the raw edge of fleece for the piping.

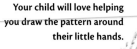

Your child will love helping you draw the pattern around their little hands.

Also Consider Lapped Seams for:

- Shoulders: Lap the back over the front.
- Armscye: Lap the garment armhole edge over the sleeve cap. (Use only if the sleeve doesn't need to be gathered to fit into the armscye.)
- Center front seam on a pullover garment: Lap the right over the left for women; lap the left over the right for men. (Right and left refer to the garment as when wearing.)
- Center back seam: Lap the garment left over the right.

Reversible Jacket

The blunt edge finish makes easy work of reversible garments. It is particularly effective on this jacket. Constructing this jacket in the traditional reversible manner would result in bulky seams and would involve turning the garment through either a side seam or a sleeve.

On the other hand, making two complete jackets, placing them wrong sides together, and finishing with a blunt edge is easy. Use a decorative blade for a pretty finish, or a straight blade for a more traditional look.

Refer to page 56 for the reversible jacket directions.

Reverse Hem Variations

MATERIALS

Solid color fleece: 1 yard

44/45" wide coordinate flannel print: 1 yard

Straight or specialty blade rotary cutter

Note: For a larger blanket, increase both the fleece and flannel yardage requirements accordingly. Cut the fleece layer 2" larger than the flannel layer.

This is an easy one! Instead of the typical garment hem, facing finish, or blanket binding, turn the hem allowance to the right side instead! You can use this wrong-side-out approach at bottom hems, sleeve hems, garment center front, and vest armhole edges.

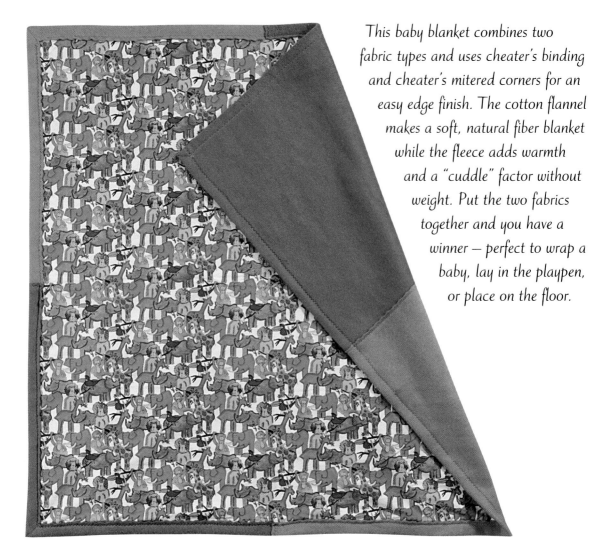

This baby blanket combines two fabric types and uses cheater's binding and cheater's mitered corners for an easy edge finish. The cotton flannel makes a soft, natural fiber blanket while the fleece adds warmth and a "cuddle" factor without weight. Put the two fabrics together and you have a winner — perfect to wrap a baby, lay in the playpen, or place on the floor.

Nancy's Note

You will notice from the flipped over corner of this blanket that I chose to piece the fleece side to have more than one color. I simply used the lapped seam technique on page 25, taped and stitched to the finished 36" x 36" dimension.

Reverse Hem Variation #1:
Cheater's Binding and Cheater's Mitered Corners

DIRECTIONS

1. Pretreat the flannel, both in the washer and dryer, to remove the inherent shrinkage. Press to remove the wrinkles. Fleece doesn't need to be pretreated (from a shrinkage standpoint), but you may choose to pretreat simply because it is going to be used for a baby.

2. Cut the fleece to 36" x 36" using a straight or specialty rotary blade. Cut the flannel 34" x 34" using a straight blade or scissors.

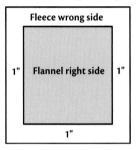

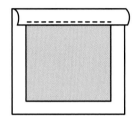

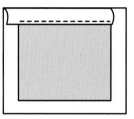

3. Lay the fleece on a table, wrong side up. (To find the right side, gently pull on the cut edge of the crossgrain [direction of most stretch]. Fleece will curl toward the *wrong* side.) Center the flannel, right side up, on top of the fleece, leaving a 1" fleece border extending beyond all the flannel edges. If necessary, trim the fleece edges so you have an even 1" border.

4. Fold a 1" fleece hem along the top edge of the blanket, encasing the flannel raw edge. Pin the hem in place, with the pins perpendicular to the hem edge. Beginning and ending at the flannel edges, edgestitch the fleece hem.

5. Trim the upper right corner of the fleece *hem* only.

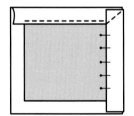

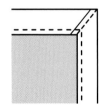

6. Fold and pin a 1" fleece hem along the right edge of the blanket, encasing the flannel raw edge. Stitch from the inner corner to the outer corner (this is the cheater's mitered corner).

7. Trim the excess fleece corner wedge piece.

8. Edgestitch the fleece side hem, stopping at the edge of the flannel.

9. Repeat this sequence to miter the remaining three corners and edgestitch the hems.

Reverse Hem Variation #2:
Cheater's Narrow Self-Fabric Binding

The cheater's self-fabric binding is a no-hassle way to achieve the look of stitched-on binding. The binding is simply a double-fold hem, folded to the right side of the blanket and edgestitched in place. Fleece's nonravel characteristic allows you to cheat when it comes to making the mitered corners.

Nancy's Note
When making a 1" double-fold binding, the blanket will finish 4" narrower and 4" shorter than the beginning fleece measurement.

DIRECTIONS

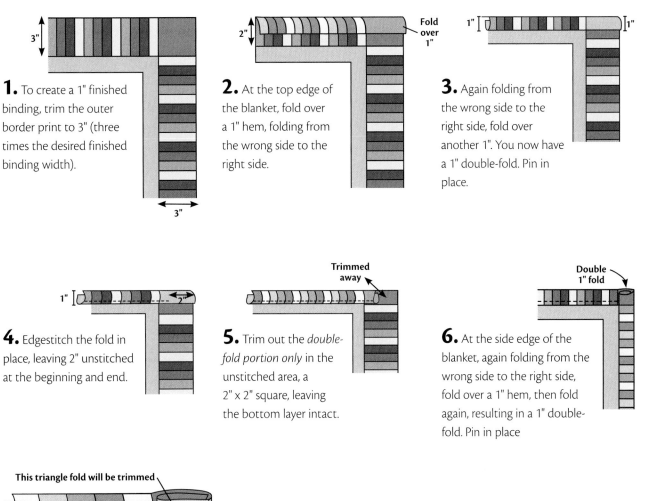

1. To create a 1" finished binding, trim the outer border print to 3" (three times the desired finished binding width).

2. At the top edge of the blanket, fold over a 1" hem, folding from the wrong side to the right side.

3. Again folding from the wrong side to the right side, fold over another 1". You now have a 1" double-fold. Pin in place.

4. Edgestitch the fold in place, leaving 2" unstitched at the beginning and end.

5. Trim out the *double-fold portion only* in the unstitched area, a 2" x 2" square, leaving the bottom layer intact.

6. At the side edge of the blanket, again folding from the wrong side to the right side, fold over a 1" hem, then fold again, resulting in a 1" double-fold. Pin in place

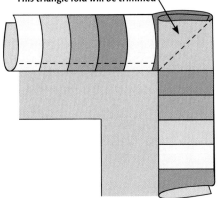

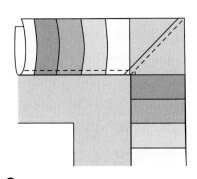

7. To make an easy mitered corner, stitch the binding from the inner corner to the outer corner.

8. Trim away the excess fleece (the wedge), cutting close to the stitching.

9. Edgestitch the side blanket binding, finishing the remaining corners and binding in the same manner.

Reverse Hem Variation #3:
Cheater's Wide Self-Fabric Binding

This is exactly the same process as Reverse Hem Variation #2 except the dimensions have changed to make a wide finished binding.

Nancy's Note
When making a 2" finished binding, the blanket will finish 8" narrower and 8" shorter than the beginning fleece measurement.

DIRECTIONS

1. Refer to the illustrations for the narrow self-fabric binding on pages 36 and 37.

2. At the top edge of the blanket, fold over a 2" hem, folding from the wrong side to the right side.

3. Again folding from the wrong side to the right side, fold over another 2", resulting in a 2" double-fold. Pin in place.

4. Edgestitch the fold in place, leaving 4" *unstitched* at the beginning and end.

5. Trim out the *double-fold portion only* in the unstitched area, a 4" x 4" square, leaving the bottom layer intact.

6. At the side edge of the blanket, and again folding from the wrong side to the right side, fold over a 2" hem, then fold again. You now have a 2" double-fold. Pin in place

7. To make an easy mitered corner, stitch the binding from the inner corner to the outer corner.

8. Trim away the excess fleece (the wedge), cutting close to the stitching.

9. Edgestitch the side blanket binding, finishing the remaining corners and binding in the same manner.

The binding can be any finished width that looks good on your project. Don't make a finished width binding narrower than ½".

To figure what beginning size to cut your blanket, add four times the finished binding width to both the length and width of the desired finished blanket size.

For a blanket with a finished size of 36" x 45" trimmed with a 2" finished binding width, cut the blanket 44" x 53" (4 x 2" finished band width, or 8" wider and longer than the finished size).

The raw edge miter is so easy. I'll never again struggle with traditional satin binding.

Blunt Edge Finish Embellishments

Blunt edge appliqués are
clean, simple, and plump.

MATERIALS FOR SCARF

Main color fleece: ⅓ yard

Contrast color fleece: ⅛ yard

Specialty blade rotary cutter

Conventional sewing machines: Leaf
template on page 151

Embroidery machines: The design
pictured is from Cactus Punch disk
SIG45, "Adventures With Fleece," Leaf 2,
outline, large size.

Blunt Edge Appliqué Methods

Blunt edge appliqué is truly a no-hassle appliqué
technique. No need for finishing satin stitches. The
appliqué can be stitched on any base fabric, as long
as the appliqué itself is fleece.

With appliqué, as with most sewing
techniques, there is always more than one way
to approach the technique and sewing tools
that make the process easier. I consider
the following notions as absolute "gotta-
haves" when it comes to easy and
successful fleece appliqué.

**Mesh transfer canvas and
water-soluble pencils**. Both of
these notions are a blessing when it
comes to transferring a motif onto
fleece for the appliqué. Refer to page
18 for transfer directions, then proceed
with either Method #1 or #2 blunt edge
appliqué technique.

**Sulky KK 2000 temporary adhesive
spray**. I love the holding power with just a light
spray of this adhesive. *Caution:* For Methods
#2 and #3, be very careful to spray only a tiny
amount of adhesive on the wrong side of the
appliqué fabric. Spray in the center of the motif,
otherwise the fleece patch will adhere in areas you
want to trim away. If your appliqué consists of multiple
areas to be trimmed (like the Paw Prints motif on page
43), pin rather than adhere the appliqué in place.

Edgestitch or edge-joining presser foot. All machine
brands offer this versatile presser foot. It has a blade in the
center, between the toes. Guide this blade along the edge of
the appliqué while setting your sewing machine needle to a left
needle position. The presser foot makes it easy to achieve consistent
edgestitching.

Appliqué scissors. The beveled edge and disc-shaped lower blade offer precision
cutting, a clean cut edge, and protection from inadvertent nicks to the base fabric.

DIRECTIONS

1. Using a decorative rotary blade, cut a scarf front from the main color fleece,
12" x 60".

2. Appliqué the leaf motifs using either the conventional or embroidery machine
methods on the following pages.

Blunt Edge Appliqué Method #1 (Conventional Machine)

▲**1.** Use mesh transfer canvas and water-soluble pencils to trace the appliqué motif onto the right side of the appliqué fleece fabric.

▲**2.** Cut out the appliqué motif.

▲**3.** Lightly spray KK2000 on the wrong side of the cutout appliqué and adhere it in place.

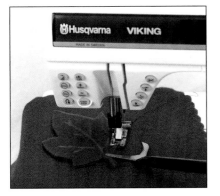

◀**4.** Edgestitch the appliqué in place using a 3mm straight stitch length and the left needle position. *Optional:* Use a machine blanket stitch or other open work decorative stitch.

Nancy's Hint
Use a stiletto to keep the appliqué flat as it approaches the needle.

Blunt Edge Appliqué Method #2 (Conventional Machine)

My Favorite!

1. For each appliqué, cut a piece of fleece appliqué fabric larger than the finished appliqué.

2. Using mesh transfer canvas and water-soluble pencils, trace the appliqué motif onto the right side of appliqué fleece fabric.

▲**3.** Lightly spray KK2000 on the wrong side of the drawn appliqué fabric and adhere or pin it in place. (See KK2000 Caution above.)

▲**4.** Straight stitch the motif using a 3mm stitch length.

▲**5.** Use appliqué scissors to trim away the excess fabric around the stitched motif, cutting close to the stitching lines.

Blunt Edge Appliqué Method #3 (Embroidery Machine)

◀**1.** Load the leaf motif from the design pack onto your machine.

2. For each appliqué, cut a piece of fleece appliqué fabric at least 2" larger all around than the finished appliqué.

3. Lightly hoop the scarf fabric with the right side facing up.

4. Lay the appliqué fleece on top of the hooped scarf with the right side facing up. Hold the appliqué fabric in place using the machine perimeter basting stitch and adhesive spray. (See the KK 2000 Caution on page 40.)

For more embroidery machine fleece appliqué techniques, refer to the book Embroidery Machine Essentials: Fleece Techniques by Nancy Cornwell.

▲**5.** Embroider the design.

6. Remove the hoop from the machine, then remove the fabric from the hoop.

▲**7.** Use appliqué scissors to trim away the excess fabric around the stitched motif, cutting close to the stitching lines.

Nancy's Blunt Edge Appliqué Hints

Hint #1: If you have a problem with the top layer of the appliqué shifting while edgestitching, lighten the pressure on your presser foot.

Hint #2: I find the dual-pronged stiletto the perfect little tool to have on hand near my machine. I use it to help guide fleece under the presser foot. It is perfect for appliqués, trim, and any situation where I need to compress fleece in front of the needle.

Hint #3: Quilt designs and appliqué designs, whether templates or machine embroidery designs, offer good simplistic motifs for blunt edge appliqué use.

Nancy's Blunt Edge Appliqué Cautions

Caution #1: Keep the motifs simple. Remember that you will be trimming the outer perimeter of the motif. Avoid busy details that would be difficult to trim. (A 10-point buck's antlers or tangled tree branches are not fun to trim.)

Caution #2: While satin stitches are the traditional edge finish for appliqués, they are not necessary or recommended for fleece. Not necessary because fleece doesn't ravel, and not recommended because the buildup of satin stitches will distort the fabric. If you want a satin stitch edge, first stabilize the base fleece fabric with an iron-on tear-away stabilizer. (For more information on how to successfully satin stitch on fleece, refer to More Polarfleece® Adventures.)

Double-Sided Appliqué Methods

This technique is one of my favorites. It is simple and very effective. The appliqués are on both sides of the blanket or scarf and are exactly back-to-back, perfectly matched. It looks like it required tedious precision work, yet it is deceptively simple.

Double-sided appliqué is exactly the same as the blunt edge appliqué Method #2 or #3, except that two pieces of fleece appliqué fabric are used, one of either side of the base fabric. Both appliqués are stitched at once!

DIRECTIONS

1. Using a wave blade rotary cutter, cut the 12" x 60" scarf front from the main color fleece, gently rounding the corners.

2. From the contrast fleece, use a straight blade to cut one strip (for a laced edge finish) exactly ⅜" wide x 60" long. Remove both selvages.

3. For *each* appliqué, cut two contrast fleece pieces at least 2" larger all around than the finished appliqué size.

4. Appliqué the paw prints motif using one of the methods on the following page.

Nancy's Note

The ¼ yard of contrast color fleece is more than you really need. The larger quantity allows you to cut bigger appliqué patches, resulting in less room for error when you are sandwiching and stitching both appliqués at once.

MATERIALS FOR SCARF

Main color fleece: ⅓ yard

Contrast color fleece (for appliqués and fleece yarn): ¼ yard

Straight and wave blade rotary cutter

Tapestry needle (with eye large enough to accommodate fleece yarn)

Conventional sewing machines: Paw Print template on page 151

Embroidery machines: The design pictured is from Cactus Punch disk SIG45, "Adventures With Fleece," Cougar, PF, large size.

Double-Sided Blunt Edge Appliqué Method #1 (Conventional Machine)

1. Use mesh transfer canvas and water-soluble pencils to trace the appliqué motif on the right side of one appliqué fleece fabric.

2. With right sides up, pin the traced appliqué piece on top of the scarf.

Nancy's Note
I pinned rather than used spray adhesive to hold the appliqué fabric in place because the adhesion would have hindered trimming between the toes.

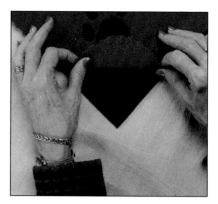

3. With wrong sides together, pin the untraced appliqué piece on the backside of the scarf, sandwiching the scarf between the appliqué pieces. (This is why the appliqué pieces are cut larger than you need. The alignment does not have to be exact.)

4. Stitch the motif, sewing through both appliqué pieces and base fabric.

5. Use appliqué scissors to trim the excess fleece from the outer edges of the stitching on both appliqué pieces, trimming close to the stitching line.

6. For the fleece yarn laced edge finish, refer to page 48 for directions.

Double-Sided Blunt Edge Appliqué Method #2 (Embroidery Machine)

1. Load the paw print motif from the design pack onto your machine.

2. Lightly hoop the scarf fleece.

3. Place the wrong side of one fleece appliqué piece against the underside of the hooped scarf fleece. Place the wrong side of the second fleece appliqué piece against the top of the hooped scarf fleece.

4. Perimeter baste or pin all three layers together.

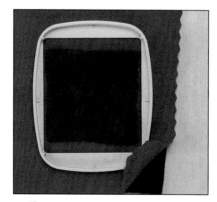

5. Embroider the paw prints.

6. Remove the hoop from the machine, then remove the fabric from the hoop.

7. Use appliqué scissors to trim the excess fabric close to the stitching line on both appliqués.

8. For the fleece yarn laced edge finish, refer to page 48 for directions.

Reverse Appliqué

Reverse appliqué with fleece is similar to traditional reverse appliqué except that when using fleece, you don't have to finish it!

Begin with two layers of fleece (like a double-layer blanket, scarf, or vest). Stitch a motif, then trim away one fleece layer within the motif.

You can combine a print with a solid fleece or use two solid fleeces.

Print and Solid Reverse Appliqué

The print and solid combination is the easiest because the fleece print gives you the motifs to stitch. Choose a print with a relatively well-defined motif to outline stitch (soccer ball, leaf, flower, animal, teddy bear, star, heart, etc.). You will be trimming that shape, so you don't want difficult nooks and crannies. Besides being difficult to trim, fussy detail is lost on fleece.

The "Hello Kitty" blanket and the Christmas throw on page 46 both feature reverse appliqué embellishment but look very different because of the prints chosen. Both blankets were first sewn and quick fringed (see page 99 for directions), then reverse appliquéd.

Take advantage of the "Hello Kitty" print to create your own design on the reverse.

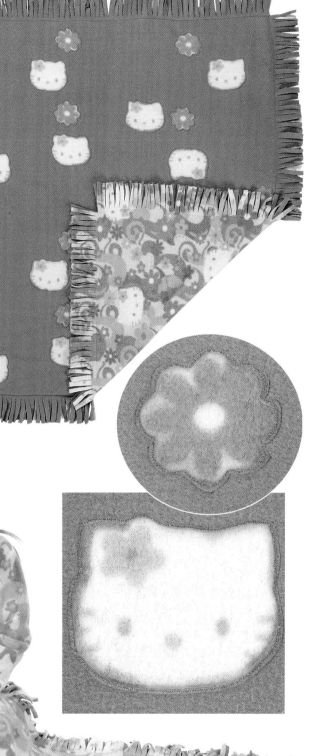

DIRECTIONS

1. Place the fleece layers with wrong sides together (finished position), stitch, and quick fringe (page 99).

2. Determine which print motifs you are going to highlight. These print motifs won't look much different on the print side but since they will be visible on the solid side, you want to make sure the look is balanced.

Nancy's Hint

If you are using an all-over print with many motifs to choose from, it is sometimes hard to decide which motifs to use. I find it a great help to lay the fleece on the floor, print side up. I place pieces of paper on top of the motifs, designating which ones to outline stitch. I can easily move the papers around, changing motifs until I get a balanced look. Then I pin the paper pieces to the motifs so I can see which are the "chosen ones" when I get to the sewing machine.

3. Stitch around the motifs, using a 3mm straight stitch.

4. Working from the solid fleece side, use appliqué scissors to trim away the solid layer only from within the stitched motif. Trim close to the stitching line.

Nancy's Comment

Decide whether the motif outline stitching should be right on the motif edge or outside the motif edge. The only way to know is to stitch a few samples and see how they look.

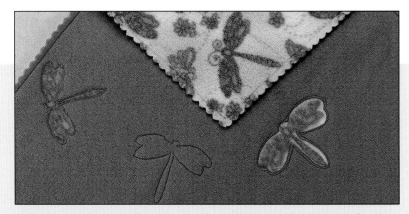

When you trim away the solid fleece layer within the stitching outline, a tiny bit of fleece remains close to the stitching line, encroaching on the print. If you sew exactly on the print outline, that tiny bit of encroaching fleece crowds the motif. If you align the outer edge of your presser foot alongside the motif's outer edge, your outline stitching will be approximately ¼" away from the motif edge. If the two fleece colors are close, you will find the trimmed motif more visible if your stitching line is at least ¼" from the motif outer edge. When the solid side is trimmed, the ground color surrounding the motif will act as a narrow border to visually frame the motif.

There is no right or wrong. It is a matter of which method best complements the motif.

Using solid colors for both layers leaves the choice of motif entirely up to you. Choose motifs with simple outlines that will be easy to trim.

Solid and Solid Reverse Appliqué

1. Use mesh transfer canvas and water-soluble pencils to transfer the motif onto the right side of one fleece layer.

2. Place the fleece layers wrong sides together (the finished position). Stitch the layers together.

3. Stitch around the motifs using a 3mm straight stitch.

4. Trim out the top fleece layer from within the motif stitching lines to reveal the contrast layer.

Trimming Options

If you trim all the motifs on one side only, it results in reverse appliqués (contrast motifs) on one side of the scarf or garment and solid, "quilted-look motifs" on the other side.

If you alternate trimming motifs (trim some from one side, some from the other), you will have contrasting reverse appliqués. (Obviously, don't trim the same motif on both sides or you'll end up with unintentional cutwork!)

Fleece Yarn

Nancy's Fleece Yarn Tips

* *Always cut the strips on the crossgrain, from selvage to selvage, in the direction of most stretch.*

* *The wider the beginning fleece strip, the thicker the resulting yarn.*

* *The width you cut the fleece depends on the end use for the fleece yarn. Never cut narrower than ³/₈" because narrow fleece will break when stretched hard.*

I introduced the concept of making fleece yarn in *Polar Magic*. I recommended fleece yarn for button loops and belt loops (perfectly matching the garment since they are made from self-fabric!), and also using the yarn as an embellishment couched in place.

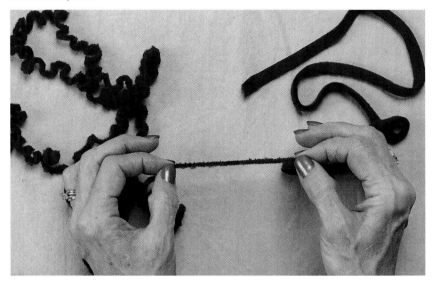

Nancy's Comment

Fleece yarn is terrific when you are looking for an exact color match for your project. However, I will be the first to admit, if all I need is a simple black or white yarn, I purchase readymade yarn for the project. It is inexpensive, consistent, and easy to use. However, if it's midnight and I'm in the middle of a creative burst of energy and need some yarn right now, I make my own.

DIRECTIONS

1. Trim and remove the fabric selvages.

2. Cut long narrow strips of fleece on the crossgrain (from selvage to selvage). Fleece strips ³/₈" wide make a versatile medium size yarn good for button loops, lightweight belt loops, or lacing for the edge of a scarf or blanket. Strips ½", ⅝", or ¾" wide make a thicker yarn good for stronger belt loops or knitting.

Nancy's Note

Yarn made from strips wider than ³/₈" won't fit through the eye of a tapestry needle.

3. Grab one end of the fleece strip and pull the strip between pinched fingers, stretching the fleece tightly. The fleece will curl and form a yarn.

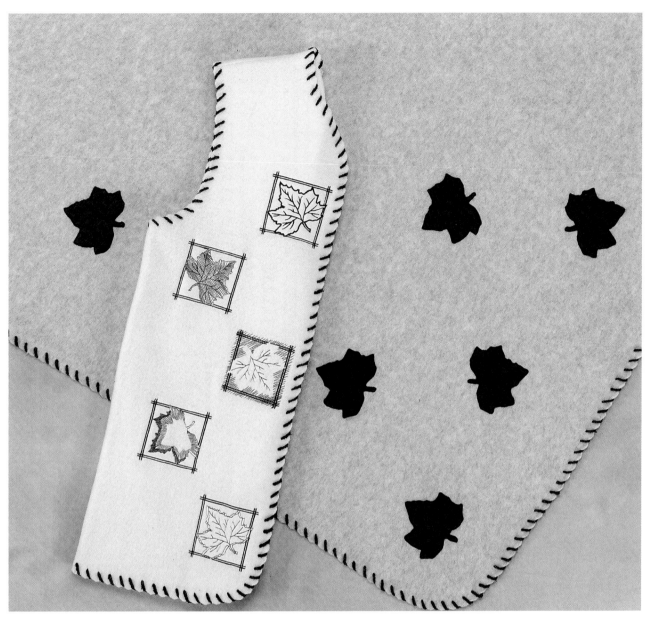

Using a wave blade to cut the main fabric provides a "stitch gauge" for lacing the yarn. This vest was featured in *Designs in Machine Embroidery* magazine. The leaf motif is from *Embroidery Machine Essentials: Fleece Techniques.*

Laced Edge

DIRECTIONS

1. Cut the scarf, vest, or blanket using a wave blade rotary cutter on those edges that are to be "laced."

2. Cut ⅜" fleece strips using a straight blade and stretch to make yarn.

3. Thread the fleece yarn through the eye of a tapestry needle.

4. Using the waves on the scarf edge as a stitch spacing guide, wrap yarn around the scarf edge.

5. Tie on a new piece of fleece yarn, cut the yarn tails, and continue wrapping the edge as necessary. Tie the ending yarn to the beginning and cut the yarn tails

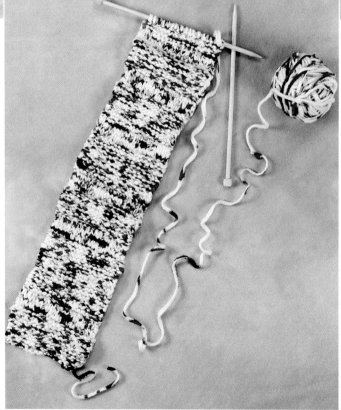

If you can make yarn from fleece, you can knit a fleece scarf!

Knitted Fleece

I met Brenda Saupe when I was presenting a fleece seminar at Ben Franklin Crafts. Brenda is a very innovative and creative sewer who works in the fabric department and she graciously showed me her clever way to make a "skein" of yarn so that she could knit (or crochet) a scarf to coordinate with her fleece garments.

The next time you buy fleece for a jacket or vest, purchase an extra yard to make fleece yarn and knit a coordinating scarf. A perfectly matching accessory every time!

Before making a skein of fleece yarn, cut and stretch a variety of strip widths to determine what thickness yarn you want for your project. Wider fleece strips create thicker yarn, which requires a larger knitting needle or crochet hook and results in a bulkier finished project.

Nancy's Note

A yard or ¾ yard of fleece yields enough yarn to make a moderate length chunky knit scarf. Since there are so many variables (how wide you cut the fleece strips, the size knitting needles or crochet hook you use, the stitch gauge), buy enough fleece to be safe. If you come to the end of your skein of yarn and find you need more, simply cut another fleece strip, stretch to make the yarn, tie on, cut the tails, and continue knitting or crocheting. Easy as that!

DIRECTIONS FOR CONTINUOUS YARN

These directions are Brenda's method for making one long continuous piece of fleece yarn. Before beginning your project, make a couple test cuts to see what thickness of yarn works for the project you have in mind. Cut strips ½", ⅝", and ¾" wide and stretch to make fleece yarn. Then choose the needle or hook size you plan to use and stitch a small piece to get an idea of the finished look. Widen or narrow the fleece strip and/or change needles or hook size until you get the look you want.

Beginning strips ½" wide, stretched into fleece yarn and knitted with size 13 (9.0mm) needles, give nice results.

1. Trim and remove the selvages from the fleece.

2. Place a strip of ½" wide masking tape along the trimmed selvage edges.

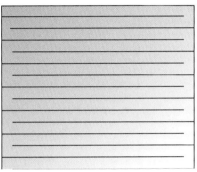

3. Using a transparent ruler and a straight blade rotary cutter, make ½" cuts, from masking tape to masking tape. Cut to, but not through, the masking tape. (The masking tape serves as a stopping point for the cuts.) If you are careful, you can skip the masking tape and just cut up to ½" from the side edges.

4. Remove the tape.

5. Beginning at the upper left corner, extend the first cut entirely through the ½" uncut edge. (This gives a starting point for making one long fleece strip.)

6. Cut through the uncut side edges, alternating sides to make one long continuous fleece zigzag.

7. Grab one end of what is now one long continous zigzag fleece strip and pull the strip between your pinched fingers, stretching the fleece firmly. The fleece will curl and form a yarn. Keep pulling until the entire long zigzag strip has been converted into one long piece of fleece yarn.

Nancy's Hint
Take your time. It's easy to get confused about which cuts to extend and which edges to leave intact. When in doubt, spread the cuts apart to see which edge to cut next. It's no big deal if you make a mistake and cut one incorrectly. After stretching the fleece strips into the yarn, simply tie the yarn ends together and cut off the tails.

Nancy's Note
You will see that there are little "ears" at each turn-around section of the yarn. Don't worry about them at this point. Wind your yarn into a skein and knit or crochet your project. In the finished project, snip off any "ears" that poke out.

Blunt Edge Idea Gallery

Horse Motif Blanket or Throw

MATERIALS

Throw (54" x 60"): 1½ yards each of print fleece and coordinate solid fleece

Blanket (60" x 72"): 2 yards each of print fleece and coordinate solid fleece

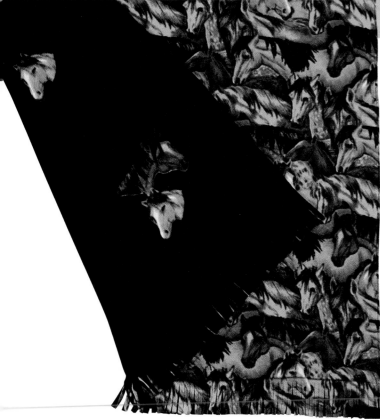

Teaming a fleece print with a coordinate solid fleece makes a cozy, double-layer blanket and coordinating pillow. This is a great gift item because you can choose a print that reflects the recipient's interest. This blanket is perfect for a horse lover, but it could just as easily have been a soccer ball print teamed with a solid team color, an autumn leaf print teamed with burnt gold, or a soft baby print teamed with a pastel solid.

DIRECTIONS

1. Sew the layers together and quick fringe them. Refer to page 98 for directions.

2. Refer to page 46 for reverse appliqué directions (choosing motifs, outline stitching, trimming).

Horse Appliqué Pillow/Multiple Pillow Sizes

For this blunt edge appliqué, I cut out the cluster of horse faces, adhered, and edgestitched. This approach made it easy to center the motifs on the pillow front.

MATERIALS

Mid-weight fleece: ¾ yard

Fleece with motifs for appliqué

20" square pillow form

Nancy's Note

The Materials and Directions given are for a 20" pillow form. (I chose a larger size to accommodate a cluster of horse faces.) The requirements for a flanged edge finish using different size pillow forms are given on page 54.

DIRECTIONS

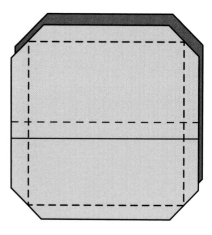

Requirements for Different Size Flanged Edge Pillows

18" Pillow Form
- Yardage: ⅔ yard
- Cut the pillow front 23" x 23" (5" larger than the pillow form)
- Trim the pillow front to 22" x 22" (4" larger than the pillow form)
- Cut two half backs 22" x 15"

16" Pillow Form
- Yardage: ⅝ yard
- Cut the pillow front 21" x 21" (5" larger than the pillow form)
- Trim the pillow front to 20" x 20" (4" larger than the pillow form)
- Cut two half backs 20" x 14" (If you have enough fleece and nap is not an issue, cut the pillow half backs with the least amount of stretch going in the 20" direction.)

14" Pillow Form
- Yardage: ⅝ yard
- Cut the pillow front 19" x 19" (5" larger than the pillow form)
- Trim the pillow front to 18" x 18" (4" larger than the pillow form)
- Cut two half backs 18" x 13" (If you have enough fleece and nap is not an issue, cut the pillow half backs with the least amount of stretch going in the 18" direction.)

1. Cut the pillow front 25" x 25" (5" larger than the pillow form).

2. Cut out the fleece motifs for the appliqués.

3. Lightly spray KK2000 on the wrong side of the cutout motifs and adhere them to the pillow front.

4. Edgestitch the motifs in place.

5. Trim the pillow front to 24" x 24" (4" larger than the pillow form).

6. Cut two pillow half backs 24" x 16".

7. Turn under and topstitch 2" hems on each half back.

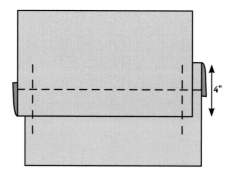

8. Overlap the half back hems 4" and baste them together at ½".

9. With right sides together, pin and stitch the pillow front to the basted half backs, using a 1" seam allowance. *Do not trim the seam allowance.*

10. Trim the corners diagonally.

11. Trim one layer from the seam allowance in the overlap area on the half backs. This makes the bulk comparable to the rest of the pillow.

12. Turn right side out. Arrange the seam allowances to lay flat.

13. Topstitch at 1", creating a 1" flange around the entire pillow.

14. Insert the pillow form.

Great Hint
Pillow forms come in a range of qualities and plumpness. When inserting the pillow form into your pillow, if the corners are not filled adequately, simply insert a small handful of polyester stuffing to plump the corner area.

Reversible Vest

This easy-to-sew vest features a decorative blunt edge finish, reverse appliqué on one side, and an outline quilted motif on the reverse side.

Choose your favorite simple vest pattern with a plain front (no seams or darts) and one-piece back. Sew the vest with side seams or redesign into a no-side-seam garment (see page 122 for directions).

DIRECTIONS

Note: Use the seam allowances given in your pattern directions.

1. Cut out the vest pieces from the main and contrast colors.

2. Sew the side seams (if needed) and shoulder seams of the main color (cream) vest.

3. Use mesh transfer canvas and water-soluble pencils to trace and draw the leaf and vine design (page 18) on the right side of the main (cream) vest. Begin at the lower edge on the left side of the garment front (as when wearing), drawing the vine up the front and over the shoulder, ending on the back. On the back, adjust the vine and add another leaf at the end as needed for balance.

4. Sew the side seams (if needed) and shoulder seams of the contrast color (taupe).

5. Place the two vests wrong sides together (finished position) and pin.

6. Sew the vests together around all the outer edges and armholes as follows:

    a. If your pattern calls for ¼" seam allowances, sew the vests together using a ½" seam allowance.

    b. If your pattern calls for a ⅝" seam allowance, sew the vests together using a ⅞" seam allowance.

7. Using the decorative scallop blade, trim close to the seamlines. (Make a test cut on a fleece scrap to make sure the blade is inserted correctly for a scallop rather than a peaked cut edge.)

8. Sewing through both layers, stitch the vine and leaf lines.

9. Use appliqué scissors to trim the main color (cream) from within the leaves.

MATERIALS

Main color fleece (cream): 1 body length (usually ¾ to 1 yard)

Contrast fleece (taupe): 1 body length (usually ¾ to 1 yard)

Scallop rotary blade

Leaf and Vine template on page 152

Reversible Shawl Collar Jacket

MATERIALS

Main color fleece (royal): yardage according to pattern

Reverse color fleece (white): yardage according to pattern

Decorative edge rotary cutter

Medium Flower template on page 151

Reversible garments are fun, warm, and offer two totally different looks in one garment. The only thing I don't like about making reversible garments is the standard method of construction, especially when using fleece. Pulling a garment through a sleeve or through a side seam opening and then hand stitching the opening closed is bulky and cumbersome when dealing with fleece. Here is another opportunity to take advantage of fleece's nonravel characteristic to reduce bulk and simplify construction.

There are many commercial patterns offering reversible coats or jackets. Choose one that has a wrap or button front and hemmed sleeves. (Zippered garments won't work as easily.) Add 4" to the sleeve length to change from a hemmed sleeve to a roll-up cuff.

DIRECTIONS

1. Using a straight rotary blade, cut out all the garment pieces from the main color fleece and the reverse color fleece. (The decorative rotary cut edge finish will be done during construction.)

2. Using a decorative blade rotary cutter, trim ¼" from the sides and top edge of the pockets.

3. Fold the top pocket facing toward the *right* side of the pocket. (The wrong side of the facing will be visible in the finished pocket.) Refer to page 31.

4. Topstitch the pocket facing in place.

5. On the wrong side of the pocket, place wash-away basting tape close to the sides and bottom cut edges. Adhere the pocket in place to one jacket layer. Edgestitch and topstitch to secure.

6. Construct the complete main color jacket following the pattern directions.

7. Construct the complete reverse color jacket following the pattern directions.

8. Pin the main color jacket to the reverse jacket, with wrong sides together (finished position).

9. With matching threads in the needle and bobbin, sew the jackets together around the entire jacket perimeter (lower edge, center fronts, upper collar, and sleeve hems) using a ½" seam allowance (on patterns with a ¼" seam allowance) or ⅞" seam allowance (on patterns with a ⅝" seam allowance).

10. Using a decorative blade rotary cutter, trim the seam allowances ¼" away from the stitching lines.

The reverse hem technique (page 34) offers a decorative alternative to the traditional pocket facing finish.

Belt

If your pattern offers one long fold-over belt, change it to a two-piece belt by adding a seam allowance along the long fold line.

1. Cut one main color belt and one reverse color belt.

2. Pin the main color belt to the reverse color belt with wrong sides together (finished position).

3. Sew around the entire perimeter using a ½" seam allowance (on patterns with a ¼" seam allowance) or ⅞" seam allowance (on patterns with a ⅝" seam allowance).

4. Using a decorative blade rotary cutter, trim the seam allowances ¼" away from the stitching lines.

Flower Embellishment

Whether you wear the main or contrast side facing out, you have a reverse appliqué flower on the left lapel and an outline-stitched flower on the right lapel.

1. Try on the jacket with the main color facing out and roll back the shawl collar as desired. Mark the placement for a reverse appliqué flower on the left lapel (left as when wearing).

2. Try on the jacket with the reverse color facing out and again mark the placement for a reverse appliqué flower on the left lapel, mirror imaging the first flower's placement.

3. Using mesh transfer canvas and a water-soluble pencil, draw one medium flower motif on each left lapel (see page 18).

4. With matching threads in the needle and bobbin, stitch the flower outlines.

5. Using appliqué scissors, trim the top fleece layer only from within the flower on each left lapel (as when wearing).

Nancy's Hint

After stitching the first flower outline, I trim away the inner layer, then I try on the jacket and double check my placement of the second flower to make sure they are even.

Whether you wear the main or contrast side facing out, you always have a "corsage" on the left lapel and a "quilted" flower on the right.

Coordinate Crusher Hat

The perfect crowning touch. The hat coordinates with the reversible jacket, no matter which jacket side is showcased.

MATERIALS

Main color fleece (royal): ¼ yard

Contrast color fleece (white): ¼ yard

Small Flower template on page 151

Large Flower template on page 151

Note: *Use a ¼" seam allowance.*

DIRECTIONS

1. From each fleece color, cut a circle 8¼" in diameter for the hat top.

2. From each fleece color, cut a band 9" wide x 24" long (with the greater stretch going in the 24" length).

3. With right sides together, sew the short ends of each band together, forming a circle.

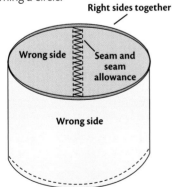

4. With right sides together and matching the center back seams, sew the bands together along one long edge. (This will become the rollback seam.)

5. Turn right side out.

6. Use mesh transfer canvas and a water-soluble pencil to trace and draw a small flower (see page 18) at the center front of the hatband and another small flower on either side of the center flower. (To determine the flower placement, roll back 3" of the contrast cuff and mark the flower placement. Unroll and trace the flowers.)

7. Stitch the flowers. On the contrast color (white) side, trim one layer only from the center of the flowers to reveal the main color (royal) peeking through.

8. Turn the band to the finished position (with the rolled-up cuff showing the flowers and the sides lying smooth

against each other). Trim approximately ¾" from the top raw edge of the outer layer (main color) to make the raw edges even. (The contrast color uses more than the main color in the rollback.)

9. Place the circle hat tops with wrong sides together and spot baste.

10. Trace a large flower in the center of the contrast (white) hat top. Stitch and trim the contrast (white) layer from within the flower to reveal the main (royal) color peeking through.

11. With right sides together, sew the hat top to the hatband. Use a 4mm stitch length and change to a size 16 needle to accommodate the bulk. Both the hat top and the rollback cuff are predominantly the contrast color (white) with the main color (royal) peeking through the trimmed flowers.

Coordinate Scarf

MATERIALS

Main color fleece (royal): ⅓ yard

Contrast color fleece (white): ⅓ yard

Scallop rotary blade

Large Flower template on page 151

Notice the "peaked" decorative edge. This is the result of using the decorative scallop rotary blade the opposite way.

DIRECTIONS

1. Cut the two scarf layers 12" x 60".

2. Place the layers wrong sides together (finished position) and cut the corners into gentle curves, using a straight blade.

3. Sew the layers together using ½" seam allowances.

4. Remove the scallop blade from the rotary handle, turn the blade over, and reassemble. (Do a test cut to make sure you have correctly changed from a scallop to a peaked cut edge.) Use the peaked edge to trim the excess fleece close to the stitching line.

5. Use mesh transfer canvas and a water-soluble pencil to draw three large flowers at the each end of the scarf (see page 18). (Refer to the photo for placement.)

6. Outline stitch the flower motifs.

7. At one end of the scarf, trim and remove the main color (royal) from within the flowers to reveal the contrast color (white) peeking through. Trim the opposite at the other end of the scarf.

Trees Jacket

This is a fun variation of the jacket pattern included in the book.

MATERIALS

Print fleece: 2 yards

Solid fleece: ¾ to ⅞ yard

Refer to page 145 for notion requirements.

DIRECTIONS

1. Using the multi-size jacket pattern included in the back of the book, cut the following:

- From print fleece

    2 front (hemmed finish)

    1 back on fold (hemmed finish)

    1 collar (plain)

    Note: *The sleeve border will be cut during construction.*

- From solid fleece

    2 sleeves (hemmed finish)

2. Determine what part of the print you want to feature on the sleeve and overlay the solid cut out sleeve with a piece of print fleece accordingly.

3. Using a 3mm straight stitch, sew the print to the solid sleeve on a dominant line of the print to create the upper edge of the border.

4. Use appliqué scissors to trim the excess print fleece, cutting close to the stitching line.

Trim the remaining print fleece to match the solid sleeve side and lower edges.

5. Baste the print to the solid along the sleeve side and lower edges using a 4mm wide x 4mm long zigzag stitch.

6. Finish constructing the jacket following the pattern directions on page 146.

I used the blunt edge appliqué technique when adding the border to the sleeve hem. The hat is the same as the Crusher Hat on page 114 except the hat top and band are a single layer of fleece.

Snowflake Reverse Appliqué Scarf

If you have my book, Embroidery Machine Essentials: Fleece Techniques, you can make this scarf on your embroidery machine. Simply use the outline stitch from the Elegant Snowflake motif. Of course, you can also use the templates in this book and a conventional sewing machine.

MATERIALS

Fleece color #1 (red): ¼ yard

Fleece color #2 (white): ¼ yard

Snowflake #1 and #2 templates on page 153

DIRECTIONS

1. Cut the two scarf layers 12" x 60".

2. Pin the fleece layers with wrong sides together.

3. Sew the layers together using a ½" seam allowance on the long sides and 5" at the short ends.

4. Use mesh transfer canvas and a water-soluble pencil to trace and draw snowflake motifs on both ends of the scarf, arranging the motifs as desired (see page 18).

5. Stitch the motifs.

6. At one end of the scarf, use appliqué scissors to trim the red fleece from within the snowflake motifs to reveal the white fleece peeking through. At the opposite end of the scarf, trim the white fleece from within the motifs to reveal the red fleece peeking through.

7. Rotary cut ¼" away from the stitching lines on the long edges of the scarf.

8. Quick fringe the scarf ends by making ½" x 5" cuts. (See page 93 for quick fringe directions.)

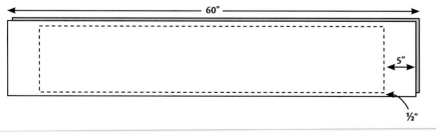

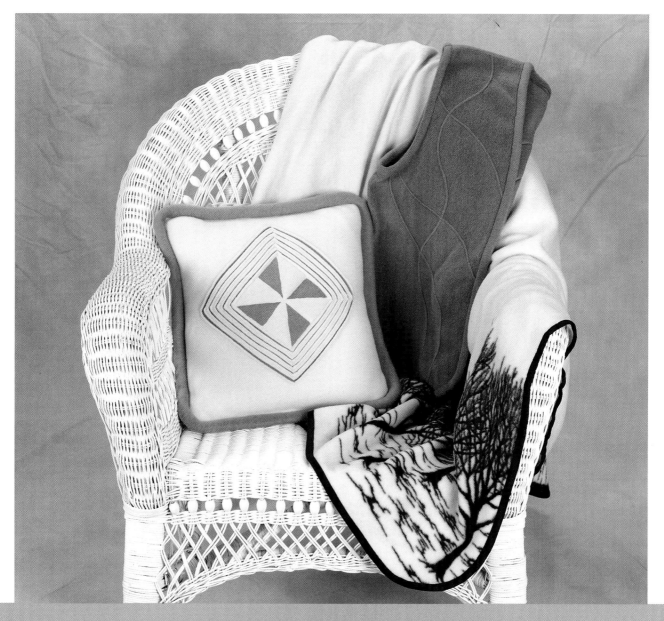

Chapter 4

Cheater's Wrapped Edge Finish

One technique with so many applications. The cheater's wrapped edge isn't a flashy technique, just a very practical one that you will use over and over again. Best of all, you can use this technique in other areas of your sewing. It is "not for fleece only." Since this is a "trim" technique, you can use this method on all kinds of fabrics (wovens as well as other knits) in all kinds of situations (garments to home dec.).

Wrapped Edge – The Cheater's Way

*In my first book,
**Adventures With
Polarfleece®**, I introduced
the cheater's wrapped edge
finish as an easy alternative
for the narrow Lycra trim
edge finish commonly used
on ready-to-wear sportswear.
Readymade garments use
Lycra trim to finish necklines,
collars, cuffs, and bottom
hems. It is a tidy, clean edge
finish that can be used in
place of rib trim.*

*Finding ribbing to match or
coordinate with fleece is often
difficult. To solve the dilemma,
fleece outerwear manufacturers
replace ribbed cuffs and
bottom bands with a narrow
binding made from nylon/Lycra
(swimwear fabric). They apply
Lycra binding using the same
method as applying cotton bias
binding to finish jewel necklines,
sleeveless armholes, and quilt
edges. I wondered why it had
to be sewn in the "traditional
binding" manner. Woven fabrics
ravel, and that's why woven
binding uses a folded edge – so
that the raw edges are enclosed.
But Lycra doesn't ravel... so
why not take advantage of that
feature?*

*And that's how the idea for
the cheater's wrapped edge
was born.*

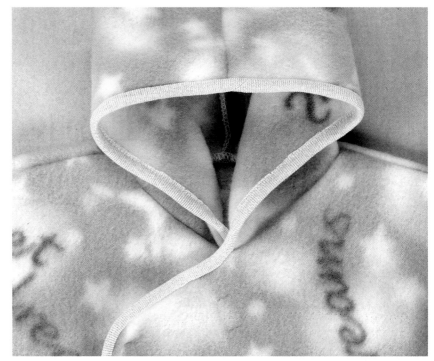

Baby bunting and wrap patterns generally call for Lycra or cotton bias trim, binding the edge in the traditional (and difficult) manner. I found a perfect color match in my ribbing yardage stash and quickly finished this bunting using the cheater's wrapped edge technique. Faster, easier, and far less bulky.

The cheater's wrapped edge is a quick, easy, good-looking, nonbulky edge finish using Lycra or any knit fabric.

DIRECTIONS

1. Cut the garment center front edge, armhole edge, sleeve edge, etc. to the finished depth.

Nancy's Note
*With a regular hem, which is turned up
and stitched, the finished edge is shorter
than the cut edge. With a wrapped edge
finish, the cut edge length or width is not
changed. The raw edge of the fabric is
simply wrapped with the trim. Therefore,
when using this technique, if there is a
seam allowance or hem allowance, cut
the garment edge to the **finished** depth.*

2. With *right* sides together, pin a *single* layer of stretch trim to the garment edge. (The stretch trim must be a minimum of four times the seam allowance width.) Keep the raw edges even.

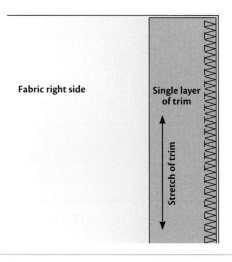

Fabric right side

Single layer
of trim

Stretch of trim

Nancy's Note

A narrow cheater's wrapped edge can be done on a conventional sewing machine, but it's better when sewn on a serger. The serger seam allowance is a consistent ¼" width and compacts the fluffy seam allowances, making it easier to wrap the trim. If a serger is not available, use a conventional sewing machine and sew a meticulous ¼" seam allowance. (How consistently you sew the ¼" seam allowance directly affects how good the finished edge will look.) To flatten the nap, zigzag stitch the seam allowance area using a 4mm wide x 3mm long stitch.

3. Sew the trim to the garment. Place the garment against the machine with the trim strip on top. Don't cut away any fabric or trim.

4. Wrap the trim strip to the *wrong* side of the garment. Wrap it up, over, and around the raw edges, encasing the trim and the fleece raw edges.

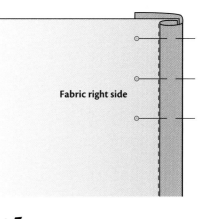

Fabric right side

5. Working from the right side of the garment, pin the trim strip in the finished position. Make sure the trim is smooth and consistent.

Nancy's Note

*The excess trim will overlap the stitching line on the **wrong** side.*

6. Sewing from the *right* side of the garment, stitch in the ditch to secure the wrapped trim strip to the backside. (Stitch in the ditch means to stitch in the previously sewn seamline.) Use an edgestitch or edge-joining presser foot for precise stitch placement.

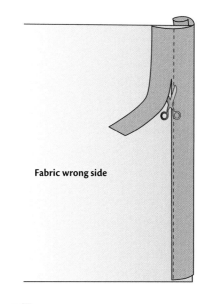

Fabric wrong side

7. Use appliqué scissors to cut the excess trim close to the stitching line on the wrong side of the garment.

The cheater's wrapped edge technique lends itself to a wide range of applications. Simply change the fabric used for the trim, or the depth of the seam allowance, or where the trim is applied, and the results are amazing. The technique is the same – only the appearance changes.

The Edge Finish Appearance Changes When You:

- substitute ribbing, a novelty knit, or fleece for the Lycra trim
- increase the ¼" seam allowance to ½", ¾", or even 1"
- use it on blankets, armholes, garment edges, or pillow edges

Trim Choices

Applying trim as an edge finish to a fleece garment or home dec item is like making a homemade sauce – you can vary the ingredients. A cheater's trim strip is similar in that the finished look can vary from application to application.

Nancy's Note

The "finished width" refers to the visible width of the trim when completed. Refer to page 67 for more information.

Lycra Trim

Lycra is available in precut 2" or 2½" widths in a variety of colors, sold packaged in precut lengths or by-the-yard on spools. You can also buy nylon/Lycra yardage (swimwear) to cut and splice your own strips.

Nancy's Note #1

I have seen narrower precut Lycra trim strips, but don't recommend them. They are just a bit too narrow, making them difficult to work with.

Nancy's Note #2

To make your own trim from swimwear Lycra yardage, cut strips 2" to 2½" wide. Refer to page 69 for directions on splicing trim strips for longer lengths.

Lycra has a shiny side and a matte side and you can use either one. Check both sides against your fabric to see which you prefer. I often find that the color on one side coordinates better simply because of the shine or lack of shine.

Use a narrow *finished* width (usually ⅜" to ⅝" wide) to finish necklines, armholes, cuffs, garment bottom edges, and blanket edges. Lycra is not often used for wider finished widths. A finished width wider than ⅝" tends to result in pull or drag lines in the trim.

Ribbing Trim

Ribbing yardage comes in a variety of widths and fiber contents. Most of the time you will have to cut and splice strips to get the length you require. Refer to page 69 for directions on splicing trim strips.

Use ribbing in a narrow *finished* width (usually ⅜" to ⅝" wide) to finish necklines, armholes, cuffs, bottom edges of garments, vest edges, and blanket edges. Wider finished widths (¾" to 1") can be used as an accent finish on the edges of vests, pillows, hats, etc. If you plan to sew dark ribbing on light-colored fleece, test the ribbing for colorfastness.

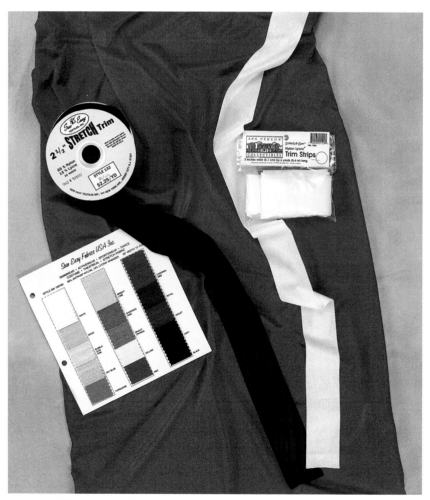

Lycra is available in precut widths as well as yardage.

Novelty Knit Trim

Interlock, jersey, panne velvet, velour, etc.

The trim for a cheater's wrapped edge can be any knit fabric – fleece, stretch velour, sweatshirting, interlock, jersey, bunting fleece, or stretch knit terry. The only requirements are that the fabric stretches and doesn't ravel.

The *finished* width can be anywhere from ⅜" to 1", depending on the look you desire for the garment or home dec item you are making.

Cut knit trim strips on the crossgrain, from selvage to selvage, resulting in the greater stretch going in the length of the strip.

When choosing knit fabrics for trim finish, consider washability, colorfastness, and stretch.

Fleece

Fleece is a great trim choice. If you are using self-fabric, the color match is perfect (obviously!).

Cut fleece trim strips on the crossgrain, from selvage to selvage, resulting in the greater stretch going in the length of the strip.

Use a conventional sewing machine to apply trim and use a wider seam allowance, usually ⅜" to ¾", resulting in a finished width of ⅝" to 1". Don't trim the seam allowance. When wrapping the fleece trim strip up, around, and over to the inside, the seam allowance plumps the wrap, giving a "piped" appearance.

Use fleece fabric for your trim when you want a plump edge finish. It's perfect for vest edges, armhole edges, pillow edge finishes, and hat trim.

Cotton ribbing provided the perfect soft look for the narrow edge finish on this vest.

Finished Width Guidelines

There are three widths to think about when doing the cheater's wrapped edge.

1. The **finished width** is the most important. It's the visible trim in the finished project.

2. The **width of the seam allowance** you use when stitching the trim strip to the garment, blanket, or pillow.

3. The **trim strip width** is how wide the starting trim strip must be in order to easily execute the wrap. Allow a *minimum* starting trim strip width of four times the seam allowance width. Wider is easier to handle.

Nancy's Note

The seam allowance dictates the necessary starting trim width.

Choosing what finished width to make the wrapped edge is fairly subjective. Where are you using it? What fabric is the trim strip? What do you want it to look like – narrow and taut, or wide and plump?

Following are the widths and applications I use the most, organized by what fabric is used for the trim strip.

Lycra Edge Finish

I find that Lycra trim is easiest to sew and looks the nicest when the finished width is between ⅜" and ½" wide.

A seam allowance of ¼" results in a ⅜" finished trim and a ⅜" seam allowance will give you finished trim ½" wide. (You gain a visual ⅛" in the turn of the fabric at the seamline and the wrap over the fleece raw edge.)

On Garments

I love to use Lycra trim as a narrow edge finish on sleeves, armholes, garment lower edges, vest outer edges, jacket fronts (before inserting the zipper), stand-up collars, edges of roll-up cuffs, and patch pocket edges.

Sew with a meticulous ¼" seam allowance (for a finished ⅜" wrapped edge). If you have a serger, by all means use it. The serger seam allowance is precise and the overlocking threads compress the seam allowance for a flat wrap finish.

On Blankets and Throws

Lycra trim offers a great blanket finish when you want an accent around the outer edges. It is a nice alternative to a blanket-stitched edge finish (and a much faster one, too!). Other fabrics can be used for the trim as long as they are lightweight and don't overpower the single-layer blanket.

Round the blanket corners to a gentle curve. (It's much easier to wrap the edges on a curve than a corner.)

Measure the perimeter of the blanket and splice strips into a longer piece, as necessary. (See page 69 for splicing directions.)

Sew the trim strip to the blanket using a conventional sewing machine and a meticulous ⅜" seam allowance (for a finished ½" wrapped edge). Don't use a serger for this step. You want a slightly wider seam allowance. If you want a bolder edge finish, sew the trim strip onto the blanket using a ½" seam allowance, resulting in a ⅝" finished trim. Test to see how the curved corners work with the wider finish.

Hold the trim taut when sewing along the straight sides of the blanket. At the curved corners, be careful not to stretch the fleece while you gently force feed the trim onto the fleece. This will allow the corner to lay flat and not buckle.

As you finish sewing the trim strip to the blanket and come back to the beginning point, stop, splice the trim ends, and then finish sewing the trim to the blanket.

Nancy's Note

In most instances, I don't sew with a seam allowance wider than ½" when using Lycra trim. Lycra trim tends to bubble and show pull lines if the finished width is much wider than ⅝". When in doubt, give it a test and see how you like it.

Fat Piping: Fleece (Self-Fabric) Edge Finish

I like to use fleece as trim because it gives a dramatic plump edge finish. (Matching self-fabric fleece offers subtlety and contrast fleece provides a bold accent.) When I introduced this technique in my *Adventures With Polarfleece®* book, I called it fat piping because that's exactly what it looks like.

Fat piping is a great self-fabric edge finish for vest edges. It is a fabulous (and super-easy) way to finish a pillow and a great finish for hatbands and cuffs.

When I use fleece as trim, I generally choose a finished width of ⅝" to ¾" for garment edge finishes and 1" for home dec use.

Because fleece is fluffy, and because you wrap over the fleece seam allowance, the finished width is noticeably wider than your seam allowance. Figure the finished width will be almost ¼" wider than your seam allowance. (It depends on the fleece thickness and how taut or loose you wrap the edge.)

Figure a minimum of four times the seam allowance depth for your beginning trim width. (Personally, when using fleece as trim, I cut the fleece trim strips five times the seam allowance width. The extra width makes it easier to handle when wrapping, pinning, and stitching.)

When using fat piping as the edge finish, plan first and sew second. Changing the order of construction may avoid the need to splice the trim ends. (Refer to page 182.)

Note: *For a variety of step-by-step application methods, refer to* Adventures With Polarfleece®.

The wandering pintuck embellishment teamed with self-fabric fat piping edge finish provide subtle interest to what would otherwise have been a plain lavender vest.

Splicing Trim

Whether you use precut Lycra trim strips or make your own trim strips from fabric, there will be times when you need to join strips to have enough trim length to complete the project.

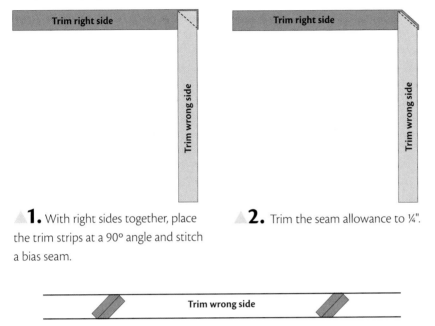

▲1. With right sides together, place the trim strips at a 90° angle and stitch a bias seam.

▲2. Trim the seam allowance to ¼".

▲3. Finger press the seam open.

4. Continue splicing strips until you have the length you need.

Use the following method when splicing on a project in progress (blanket edge finish, fat piping pillow edge, etc.).

1. Begin stitching the trim strip 3" to 4" from the actual end of the strip.

2. When approaching the end of the trim (the splice area), judge how much trim length you need. Pin the ends at a 90° angle and stitch the bias seam.

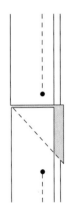

▲3. The amount of unsewn trim will vary according to the trim width you use.

Refer to page 139 to see this in "real life."

Nancy's Hint

When splicing trim, always pin the bias seam first, then turn the strip to the finished position to see if you arranged the fabrics correctly. (If wrong, it's so much easier to unpin than to rip out!)

I took great advantage of fleece's nonravel characteristic when making this vest: raw edge collar, capped yoke seam, raw edge pocket, fleece rickrack embellishment, and fat piping armhole finish.

More Ideas for Cheater's Wrapped Edge

The cheater's wrapped edge is one of those clever, yet simple techniques that takes on a life of its own. The more you use it, the more ways you find to use it.

**Fat piping is a great edge finish for fleect hats.
For step-by-step directions, see page 114.**

Nancy's Note

Not for fleece only! The cheater's wrapped edge is an edge finish that can be applied to any fabric. It is the trim strip that needs to be a knit, but you can put it on anything!

**The no-side-seam
chenille vest. Self-
fabric fat piping is an
easy way to finish the
vest edges without
detracting from the
surface interest of the
chenille. For step-by-step
instructions, see page 122.**

For step-by-step directions, see page 128.

Wrapping the edges of pillows is a great way to coordinate with a blanket. For step-by-step directions, see page 137.

Chapter 5

Chenille

Chenille is a terrific sewing technique that captured everyone's heart when Nanette Holmberg introduced Faux Chenille to the sewing world. It is a unique technique done on ordinary fabric, yielding unexpected results.

Faux Chenille is a great texturizing technique traditionally performed on woven fabrics such as rayon, cotton, denim, or muslin to mimic the texture of old-fashioned chenille bedspreads popular in the 1930s, '40s, and '50s. As many as six layers of fabric are stacked on each other and stitched together with multiple rows of straight stitching lines done on the bias. Then, using a rotary cutter, all the layers except the bottom one are slashed open between the stitching lines. The cut raw edges are then "roughed up" with a special brush or with your fingers. The stitched-and-slashed fabric is then tossed in the washer and dryer. When laundered, the cut edges fray to take on a ruffled appearance, creating the chenille look.

When Nanette Holmberg developed her famous Faux Chenille, I doubt she even gave a passing thought to applying this fun technique to fleece. The nonravel characteristic of fleece, combined with its lofty nature, is what inspired me to attempt "chenilling" fleece.

Fleece chenille is similar to Faux Chenille but the easy nature of fleece allows you to simplify the process. Although fleece chenille looks intricate, it is a very simple technique. Best of all, it offers tremendous potential for embellishment and surface interest.

Chenille adds interest to garments, accessories, and home déc.

Fleece Chenille Basics

When I began experimenting with the concept of fleece chenille, it was immediately obvious that six layers were not needed. The sunken stitches of the channels on the loft of two fleece layers provided enough tension to produce a lovely "bloom."

- Select a high quality mid-weight fleece. Lightweight fleece doesn't have enough thickness to produce a rich fluffy bloom. And since you are using two layers of fleece, a heavyweight fleece would be too bulky. Mid-weight fleece works best. (Which is good because most fleece yardage found in fabric stores is mid-weight.)
- For the most effective chenille, choose medium to strong contrasting fleece colors. Subtlety is lost in the loft and nap of fleece. The stronger the contrast, the more noticeable and dramatic the chenille effect.

• Experiment and play. Place the lighter solid color on top and a darker solid color underneath. Stitch a few channels and slash them open. Reverse the process by placing the darker color on top and the lighter color underneath. Study the results and choose whichever best suits your taste and intent.

• Combining a fleece print with a coordinate fleece solid dramatizes the print with texture.

• Adjust the stitch length to 3mm to 3.5mm.

• Sew rows of channel stitching on the bias (diagonal). Channels sewn on the straight-of-grain or crossgrain tend to lay closed when slashed open.

• If choosing a multi-directional stitching motif (to echo in rows and rows of stitching), choose a design that will have at least half or more of the channels on the bias.

• Keep the channels narrow. For best results, sew channels ⅜" or ½" apart. When the channels are slashed open, releasing the tension on the top layer of fleece, the cut edges bloom to reveal the contrast layer underneath. Wider channels will have less tension, and therefore less bloom.

• Layers can be arranged wrong sides together or with both right sides facing up. It depends on whether the unslashed layer will be seen in the finished project.

Nancy's Caution

Since there is such a variety of fleece qualities, densities, thicknesses, and naps, make a test sample to see how your chosen combination of fleeces is going to bloom using both ⅜" channels and ½" channels. My personal preference is stitching the rows ⅜" apart. This spacing seems to give the most consistent bloom on the widest variety of fleeces.

Nancy's Hint

If you are having a difficult time spacing your ³/₈" stitching lines accurately and consistently, try moving your needle to the far right needle position and aligning the left edge of the presser foot along the previously sewn stitching line.

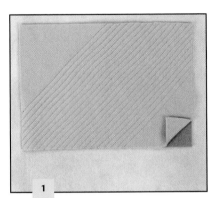

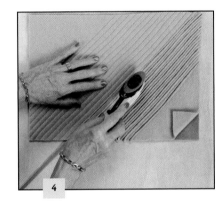

- Use Omnigrid Mini Omnistrips for easy, accurate slashing. An easy way to slash the upper layer on straight rows is to insert a Mini Omnistrip. These mini cutting mats are easy to use and protect the bottom layer from being cut.
- Sew the channels ⅛" wider than the width of the mini cutting strip you will use. Space the stitching lines ⅜" apart when using the ¼" mini strip and ½" apart when using the ⅜" mini strip.

Nancy's Note

There are wider cutting strips available, but these are better suited to making chenille on woven fabrics. (Remember, fleece blooms best with narrow channels.)

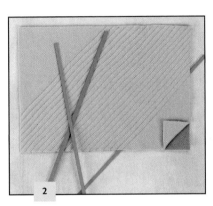

Electric scissors make quick, easy, and efficient work of slashing the upper fleece layer to create fleece chenille. Simply insert the bottom prong between the fleece layers and slice the top layer. It's very easy to "steer" and easy to see where you are going.

If you have electric scissors, you can easily make interesting chenille designs involving curved channels. The mini strips limit you to slashing open straight channels because the strips don't bend around curves. However, with the short blades of the electric scissors, you can easily slash open channels that are flowers, hearts, waves, etc. For the prettiest bloom, make sure that half or more of your channels are sewn on the diagonal.

Chenille Yardage

Make the chenille yardage first and cut out the pattern pieces second. Layer larger-than-needed pieces of fleece and stitch the channels. Then cut out the pattern pieces and slash the channels open. Although the layering, stitching, and slashing does not itself alter the size of the fabric, with all the stitching lines there is inherent shifting of layers.

I always make my fleece layers a respectable amount larger than the actual dimensions I need. Invariably I find that my beginnings and endings tend to get a little sloppy. With a larger piece, I can place my pattern piece in the prettiest chenille area.

Using chenille yardage, you can create chenille yokes, sleeves, garment backs, collars, pillow tops, etc.

Keeping the rows straight: As you work your way through the multiple rows of stitching for chenille yardage, no matter how careful you are you will soon find yourself getting a bit off-kilter. To help keep your stitching lines straight and at a consistent angle, draw some guidelines on the fleece before you begin stitching.

Using a water-soluble pencil, draw the first bias line at a 45° angle. Draw additional parallel guidelines 3" apart. As you sew rows and rows of stitching lines, the guidelines help keep you on the right track.

If you find yourself off-kilter, gradually alter the stitching lines to get back to the correct angle. Don't try to accomplish the correction in one or

Using water-soluble pencils to draw guidelines helps keep your stitching rows on track.

two rows of stitching (that would be too obvious).

If your machine balks at feeding the fleece layers under the presser foot, first lengthen the stitch length. If the longer stitch length doesn't help the situation, lessen the pressure on the presser foot.

Chenille Strips

Did you know that chenille is the French word for caterpillar? I thought about calling this technique the "fleece caterpillar" but decided that "chenille strips" was more appropriate.

The popularity of traditional chenille keeps growing, with different applications and variations. It grew into chenille embellishment by Fabric Café, Chenille-by-the-Inch. Chenille strips are a fleece version of Chenille-by-the-Inch.

Use chenille strips as surface embellishment on pillows or garments, to make appliqués, or to represent a flower stem or vine as shown on this blanket.

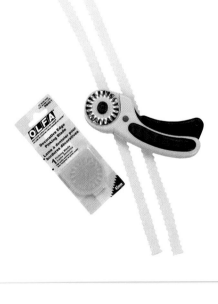

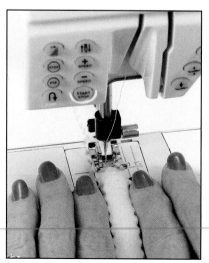

DIRECTIONS

1. Using a *pinking* blade rotary cutter, cut two ½" x 60" strips of fleece (with the greater stretch going in the length).

2. With *wrong* sides facing up, lay one pinked strip on top of the other. Using a stretch stitch or a narrow zigzag (2mm wide x 2.5mm long), stitch the layers together, sewing down the center of the strips.

Nancy's Hint
For an easy way to keep the strips together while stitching, place your index fingers alongside both sides of the presser foot to form a tunnel to feed the strips under the presser foot.

3. Stretch the fleece firmly, drawing it through your pinched fingers. The fleece will curl on itself and form a long "fuzzy caterpillar" chenille strip.

4. Place wash-away basting tape on the back (flat) side of the chenille strip. Adhere the chenille strip where desired. Stitch the strip in place by sewing down the middle of the strip, using a 4mm long straight stitch.

Blunt edge, dimensional and chenille flower appliqués garnish the chenille strip stem and leaves. For step-by-step directions for this blanket, see page 116.

Chenille Idea Gallery

Jaguar Jacket

The gorgeous Jaguar Jacket featured on the book cover was the obvious choice for the first chenille project. I've always admired the gorgeous chenille sleeves quilters put in their jackets and knew that fleece chenille would provide the same drama in a fleece garment.

I am constantly asked, "What pattern did you use?" Well, this time the answer is easy — the pattern is included at the back of the book!

Refer to Chapter 8 for the pattern's ease factors, the basic construction directions, and optional collar, sleeve, and hem finishes. Below are the components to combine with the basic construction directions to make the Jaguar Jacket.

MATERIALS

Print fleece: 2 yards

Solid fleece: ¾ to ⅞ yard (for sleeve under layer)

Refer to page 145 for notion requirements

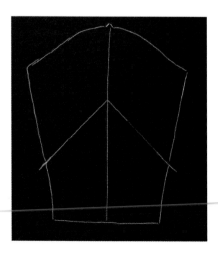

DIRECTIONS

1. Cut the following:
- From print fleece
  - 2 fronts
  - 1 back (on fold)
  - 1 piece for polar ribbing collar (refer to page 146 for dimensions)
  - 2 pieces for sleeves, 3" larger all around than sleeve pattern piece
    - (6" additional width and height)
- From solid fleece
  - 2 pieces for sleeves, 3" larger all around than sleeve pattern piece
    - (6" additional width and height)

2. Use a water-soluble pencil to draw a rough outline of the sleeve pattern piece on the *wrong* side of the *solid* color sleeve piece. Match the pattern's straight-of-grain and stretch arrows to the fleece's straight-of-grain and greater degree of stretch. Draw the sleeve centerline. Draw one chevron line somewhere in the middle of the sleeve piece, extending the chevron a little beyond the sleeve outline. (Use the 45° angle marking on your clear ruler.)

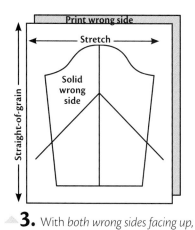

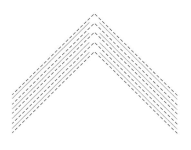

----- Dashed line = Stitching line
―――― Solid line = Slashed open between
stitching lines – uncut at apex

3. With *both wrong sides facing up,* place the solid sleeve piece on top of the print sleeve piece. Double check that the right side of the print is against the table and the wrong side of the solid is facing up. (You don't want to do all that stitching and find out it is wrong!)

5. Using a 3mm stitch length and matching thread in the needle and bobbin, stitch the drawn chevron line. Stitch subsequent rows parallel to each other and spaced exactly ⅜" apart until the sleeve outline is completely filled. Use the drawn centerline as the pivot point. Begin and end the stitching rows beyond the drawn sleeve outline. There is no need to backtack at the beginning and ending. Repeat on the second sleeve.

6. Using the sleeve pattern piece, cut out the sleeves from the chevron-stitched double-layered fleece. Align the sleeve center to the drawn centerline/pivot points.

4. Using a very long stitch length and sharply contrasting threads in both the needle and bobbin, baste the layers together down the centerline, extending above and below the drawn sleeve outline. Baste another line on either side of the centerline. Pin the layers together around the edges. (These basting lines will discourage the fabric from shifting during the stitching process and the long stitch length and contrast thread colors make them easy to remove when finished.)

7. With the jaguar print side facing up, either insert a ⁵⁄₁₆" Omni Ministrip cutting mat in each channel or use electric scissors to carefully slash the print channels open, centering the slash cuts in each channel. Cut up to but not through the pivot point (approximately ½" at the pivot point of the channel will remain uncut).

To make the polar ribbed collar and to construct the jacket, refer to page 146 for directions.

Nancy's Note

I chose not to slash the channels at the pivot point. I was concerned that since this was on the outer edge of the sleeve, wearing the jacket might cause the tips of the chevron points to curl over, so I decided to cut up to approximately ¼" of the pivot point. Although my reason for not slashing open in entirety was purely practical, the result was dramatic and beautiful. The uncut narrow furrow running from the shoulder to the sleeve hem gave the added benefit of looking like a fur pelt line!

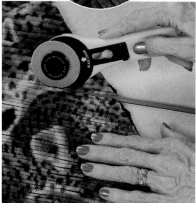

Basket Weave Scarf

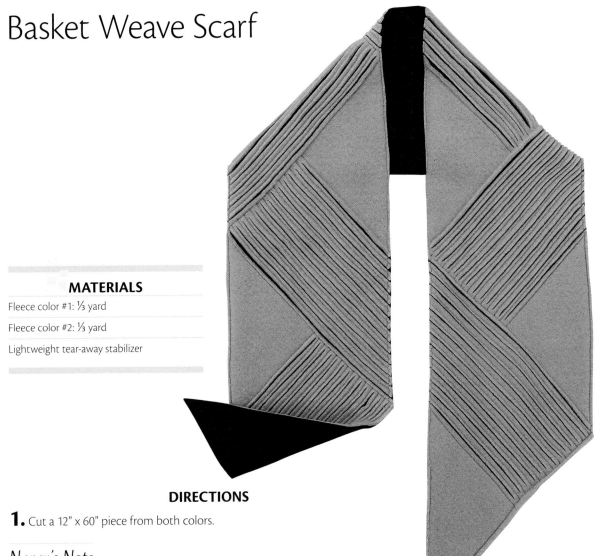

MATERIALS

Fleece color #1: ⅓ yard

Fleece color #2: ⅓ yard

Lightweight tear-away stabilizer

DIRECTIONS

1. Cut a 12" x 60" piece from both colors.

Nancy's Note
The finished scarf width will be approximately 8½". The extra beginning width allows for any fabric shifting that may occur during the chenille stitching process.

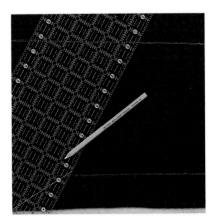

2. On the right side of one of the scarves, draw lines 8" apart, running the length of the scarf.

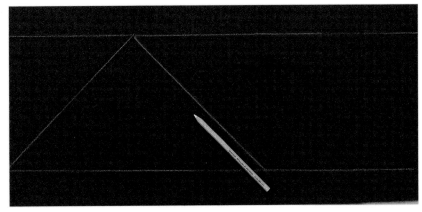

3. On mesh transfer canvas, draw an upside down "V" 8" high x 16" wide. Beginning at the left end of one layer of the scarf, use the traced mesh and a water-soluble pencil to draw an upside down "V."

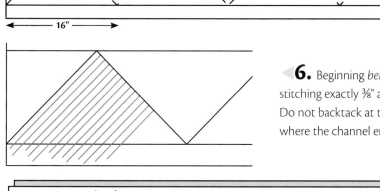

4. Slide the mesh and draw another upside down "V." Continue until you have drawn 3½ "V"s. (You end with an upswing to complement the beginning scarf end.)

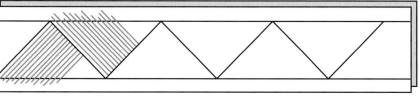

5. Place the scarf layers wrong sides together (right sides facing out). Stitch on the drawn zigzag line.

6. Beginning *below* the drawn scarf width line, stitch 13 rows of stitching exactly ⅜" away from and parallel to the first leg of the zigzag. Do not backtack at the beginning of the stitching, but do backtack where the channel ends at the next zigzag leg.

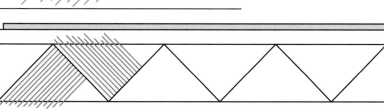

7. Beginning *above* the drawn scarf width line, stitch 13 rows of stitching exactly ⅜" away from and parallel to the second leg of the zigzag line. Continue stitching parallel rows for rest of the zigzag line.

8. Cut the scarf to 9" wide (½" beyond the stitched triangle points). Cut the scarf ends ⅛" to ¼" away from the angled stitched lines.

9. Slash open the channels to create the chenille bloom.

10. Stitch the scarf layers at the long side edges with ½" seam allowances. (To keep the chenille cuts laying flat while stitching over them, lay a small strip of lightweight tear-away stabilizer on top of the scarf edge before stitching.)

11. Trim close to the stitching (⅛" to ¼" away from the stitching line, as desired).

12. Remove the stabilizer from the stitching.

Diamond Chenille Scarf

MATERIALS

Fleece color #1 (white): ¼ yard

Fleece color #2 (red): ¼ yard

DIRECTIONS

1. Cut a 9" x 60" scarf from both colors.

2. Draw a 5½" square on mesh transfer canvas.

3. Use a water-soluble pencil to draw a centerline down the entire length of the right side of one scarf.

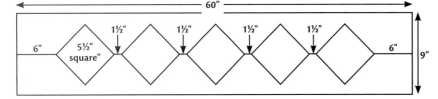

4. Rotate the square paper template to form a diamond and center it over the drawn centerline. Beginning 6" from one scarf end, draw five diamonds on the scarf, spacing them 1½" apart. Trim the other end of the scarf to 6" beyond the last diamond.

5. Pin the scarves wrong sides together. With matching thread in the needle and bobbin, sew the first traced diamond. Sew a second row of stitching exactly ⅜" away from and inside the first stitching line. Repeat stitching rows for a total of seven stitching lines (creating six channels).

6. Finish by stitching two short lines across the remaining small center diamond.

7. Repeat for the remaining four diamonds.

8. Stitch the long side seams of the scarf with ⅜" seam allowances, beginning and ending 4" from the ends of the scarf.

9. Using a rotary cutter, trim the long sides of the scarf close to the seamline.

10. To make a starting point for the chenille cuts, use appliqué scissor points to cut a small slit in the outermost channel of the first diamond. Cut the top fleece layer only.

11. Insert a ⁵⁄₁₆" mini strip in the channel and cut the channel open using a rotary cutter. Lift the mini strip at the point and slide it into the next channel. Repeat until all the diamond channels have been slashed open. Use the points of appliqué scissors to slash the innermost channels.

12. Trim the scarf ends even.

13. Quick fringe the scarf ends, making fringe cuts ½" wide x 4". (Refer to page 93 for quick fringe directions.)

Chenille Robe

The light-hearted spirit of this print presented many options for a "little girl" ensemble. I first thought, "What a fun robe!" Then I decided the robe needed a pint-sized coordinate blanket (see page 103). Then a coordinate chenille tote was needed to pack up the robe and blanket to go to Grandma's for a sleepover.

I decided on the chenille embellishment first, then set out to find an appropriate robe pattern. However, no pattern gave me an obvious place to use chenille, so I adapted the pattern to suit my desires!

The following thought processes give you an idea of how to tweak a pattern to provide the embellishment area you want.

Cuffs

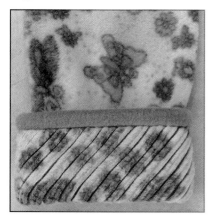

casing, I made the solid color fleece under layer extend ¾" above the chenille yardage, folded it over the edge of the chenille cuts, and edgestitched it in place to finish the cuff edge.

Then I sewed the finished chenille cuff onto the sewn sleeve. With both wrong sides facing out, I stitched the cuff to the sleeve hem. When turned to the finished position, the chenille cuff became the new rollback cuff.

The cuffs were the perfect place to showcase a chenille accent. And easy to adapt to a sew-on rollback cuff.

Cut the sleeve length at the finished hem length plus the construction seam allowance (¼" or ⅝"). Draw a separate sew-on cuff 3½" high x the lower sleeve width.

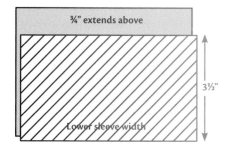

¾" extends above

3½"

Lower sleeve width

Fabric wrong side

Fold over hem stitching line

wrong side

First make chenille yardage and cut the new separate cuffs from the yardage. I finished the top edge of the cuff the same as the chenille tote bag on page 85, step 12. Using the same approach as the tote's upper fold-over

Chenille Lapel

The tricky part came when I wanted to put chenille on the robe's lapel. Like most shawl collar robes, the collar shape was "cut-on" to both the robe front and front facing as opposed to a separate sewn-on collar piece. That meant the visible portion of the shawl was in reality the facing folded back, which posed a problem. Sometimes the facing was the facing (below the waist) and sometimes the facing was the robe (the turn-back shawl).

How was I going to chenille some but not all? Where was I going to put the solid under layer?

Using the robe front facing pattern piece, I folded the collar to the finished position, and drew that fold line on the facing pattern piece. I marked the straight-of-grain line in the shawl area as well as a 45° angle line for the beginning chenille stitching line.

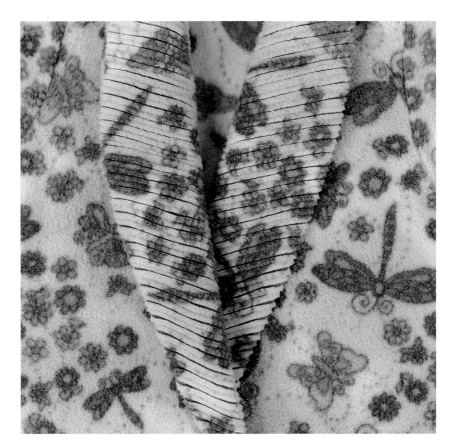

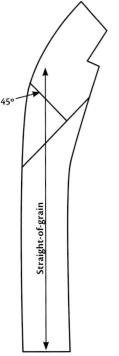

45°

Straight-of-grain

I then overlaid the collar area with pattern tracing material and drew a separate collar section, drawing in the straight-of-grain line and angled line. Now I had a specific collar area to "chenille."

I used my new chenille collar pattern piece to cut a solid color fleece for the chenille under layer. I then placed the solid color under layer piece under the robe facing, basted it in place, and stitched bias rows of stitching for the chenille. (That's why the straight-of-grain lines are important. With the unique shape of a shawl collar, it would be difficult to determine the bias.)

After "chenilling" the fold-back collar area of the facing, I simply followed the pattern construction directions to make the robe.

Nancy's Comment

I think I spent more time determining where to "chenille" than I spent constructing the rest of the robe! But the result was worth it!

Belt

The belt was by far the easiest decision to make and the quickest to sew. I took advantage of fleece's nonravel characteristics and used the blunt edge finish.

I placed two half belts wrong sides together (the finished position), stitched them together with a ½" seam allowance, and rotary trimmed close to the stitching line. Neat. Quick. And easy!

Coordinate Chenille Tote

After making the robe and rag quilt (see page 103 for the quilt directions), I decided a coordinating tote would add a nice finishing touch to the ensemble.

DIRECTIONS

1. Cut the following:
- From print fleece
    - 8½" circle (for the base)
    - 30" x 18" (for one side panel, with the stretch in the length)
- From solid fleece
    - 8½" circle (for the base)
    - 30" x 20" (for one side panel, with the stretch in the length)

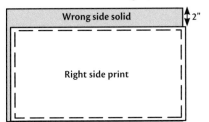

2. Place the print rectangle against the solid panel with wrong sides together. Position the print panel on the solid so that 2" of the solid panel extends above the print panel. Baste the pieces together.

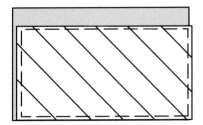

3. On the right side of the print panel, draw 45° angle lines, spaced approximately 3" apart.

4. Use the drawn lines as a guide to stitch rows ⅜" apart. Sew from the top basted edge to the lower edge, filling the fabric piece.

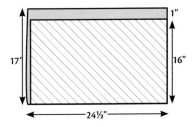

5. Refer to the illustration to cut the rectangle. Remove the remaining basting stitches.

6. Create chenille by slashing open the channels on the print side. (Refer to page 75 for directions.)

7. Cut a circle 8" in diameter from stabilizer.

MATERIALS

Fleece print: ½ yard

Fleece solid: ⅝ yard

Stiff heavyweight sew-in stabilizer (for bottom base): ¼ yard

Draw cord or ribbon: 1¼ yards

Buttons, cord locks, or pony beads as desired (to decorate draw cord ends)

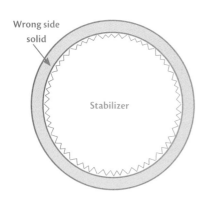

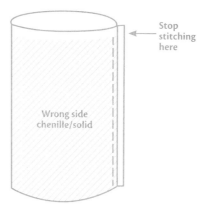

▲**8.** Using a wide and long zigzag stitch, center and stitch the stabilizer to the wrong side of the solid base.

9. Sew the print base to the solid base with wrong sides together (sandwiching the stabilizer), using a ¼" seam allowance.

▲**10.** With right sides together, sew the chenille side panel into a circle, using a ¼" seam allowance. Sew from the bottom of the panel up to, *but not through*, the solid extension.

▲**11.** With right sides of the print together, sew the side panel to the stabilized base as follows:
- Divide the base perimeter into quarters and mark with pins.
- Divide the chenilled edge of the side panel into quarters and mark with pins.
- Match the quarter marks of the base to the quarter marks of the side panel.
- Sew the base to the side panel using ¼" seam allowances.

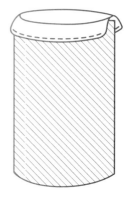

▲**12.** At the top edge of the tote, fold the solid facing (1" extension) onto the print fleece, encasing the raw edge of the chenille and at the same time forming a casing for the draw cord. Edgestitch the facing to the tote bag, beginning and ending at the unsewn ends of the folded-over facing.

13. Insert decorative ribbon or cord in the casing and cut it to the desired length. Add decorative beads, buttons, or cord locks, as desired, to the ends of the draw cord.

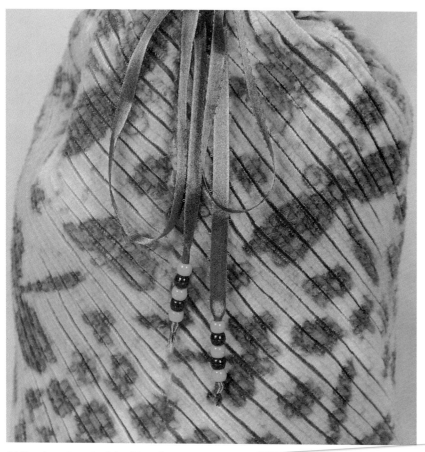

Add beads to the ends of the ribbon draw cord.

Chenille Appliqué

Using chenille as an appliqué is a fun way to embellish readymade as well as constructed items. If you apply it to a readymade item, make sure you have accessibility. You will need to be able to completely turn the item in all directions under the presser foot. Consider chenille appliqué for a garment front, back, pillow top, or purse embellishment.

Fleece chenille can be applied to any fabric because it is the appliqué itself that is fleece.

DIRECTIONS

1. Use transfer mesh and a water-soluble pencil to draw the heart design on the right side of the fleece appliqué fabric. Draw a centerline through the heart to use as a guide for pivoting the stitching at the points. (Do *not* cut out the heart shape.)

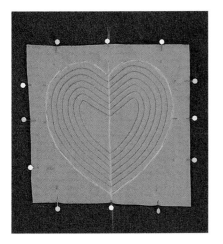

2. Place the drawn fleece appliqué on the garment or home dec item and pin it in place.

3. Beginning at one side of the heart, stitch the design. (Begin and end at one side of the heart, with the ending stitching running over the beginning stitching. Don't begin at either the top or bottom point of the heart because the overlapping beginning and ending stitches will be more noticeable at these places.)

Nancy's Note

Only the appliqué itself needs to be fleece. The base garment or home dec item can be any fabric (as illustrated here with the denim shirt). When making your own appliqué, allow for the beginning fleece appliqué piece to be at least 1" larger all around than the actual motif.

APPLIQUÉ MATERIALS

Fleece for heart appliqué: 12" x 12"

Heart template on page 154

4. Stitch a second row exactly ⅜"
away from and inside the heart outline
stitching. Repeat this step five more
times, resulting in seven stitched lines
and six channels.

5. Slash open the channels, carefully
cutting only the fleece appliqué layer.

Nancy's Note

*Electric scissors makes slashing the curved
channels quick and easy. If you don't
have electric scissors, cut the channels
open using the points of your appliqué
scissors. Slash slowly and carefully,
cutting as evenly as possible.*

6. Using appliqué scissors, trim and
remove the excess fleece from the outer
edge of the heart and from within the
unstitched center of the heart.

**The Quilter's Pillow center features reverse appliqué.
A simple change of direction for the chenille channels
results in two very different looks.
See page 128 for directions.**

Embroider a pillow top and use fleece chenille to
frame the design. I first stitched the embroidery
design (from the Brother Pacesetter Card #20,
"Lace Designs") on the white fleece pillow front,
then placed red fleece behind the pillow front. I
sewed multiple rows of diagonal stitching lines to
"frame" the motif and slashed open the channels.
See Quilter's Pillow on page 128 for directions.

More Ideas for Chenille

This purple and lavender scarf is one of eight scarves in my "Polar Magic" pattern #4263 for McCall Pattern Co., available in fabric stores. It pairs dark and light purple and features a band of zigzag stitching rows down the center of the scarf.

I designed the snowflake jacket, hat, and mitten ensemble for McCall Pattern Co. The September 2004 pattern #4666 has accents of fleece chenille and polar ribbing.

Photo courtesy of McCall Pattern Co.

These scarves were featured in the October 2003 issue of *Sew News* magazine. The Candy Cane scarf got its name because of the colors used. The two-layer scarf is filled with diagonal stitching lines. To get the candy cane effect, I simply slashed open a series of channels, alternating sides. There may be times when you would like to incorporate a third color into the mix. The Spirit Scarf sandwiches white fleece between layers of red and blue. The three layers were filled with diagonal stitching lines. Channels on both sides were then slashed using the intact center white layer as a base.

Nancy's Caution

As soon as you incorporate a third layer of fleece into your project, you add a significant amount of bulk. Make sure your chosen fleece is not too thick or too bulky when stacked in three layers.

The popular crusher style hat is one of my favorites because it is a terrific example of how to effectively incorporate a variety of fleece techniques into one project. The directions for the hat are given on page 114.

Chapter 6

Quick Fringe

Quick fringe is another blunt edge technique. It is one of those ideas that makes you say, "Why didn't I think of that before?" It's very simple, very quick, and very effective. I have included the quick fringe technique in all my books, but in this book its use has expanded so dramatically that it warranted its own chapter.

Quick Fringe Basics

- Fringe cuts can be virtually any width. The most common and most effective are fringe cuts between ½" and 1" wide.

- Unless you have a specific design need, never cut fringe narrower than ½" when the fringe is cut on the crossgrain (fringe cuts perpendicular to the selvage). Fringe cuts on the crossgrain are stretchy. Narrow stretchy fringe cuts distort easily.

- Never cut fringe narrower than ½" on baby or toddler items. Narrower fringe can potentially break off and present a swallowing danger.

- Fringe cuts can be virtually any length. The most common (and most effective) are between 2½" and 5" long.

- Quick fringe cuts can be made using a straight or specialty blade rotary cutter.

- The width and length of the fringe and the choice of blade edge are governed by the end use, the fleece print, and personal taste. There is no right or wrong.

Quick Fringe Technique

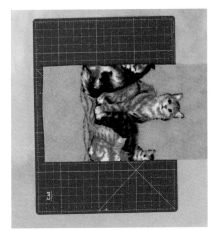

1. Lay the fleece edge to be fringed on top of a large cutting mat.

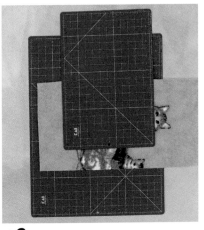

2. Lay a smaller cutting mat on top of the fleece, sandwiching the fleece between the two mats. Position the smaller mat so the edge to be fringed extends beyond the small mat edge.

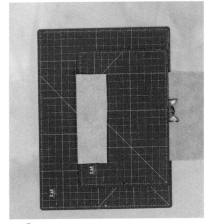

3. Fold the fleece to be fringed back onto the smaller cutting mat, using the grid lines to judge the depth of the fringe and alignment of the cuts. Keep the fleece taut against the small mat edge.

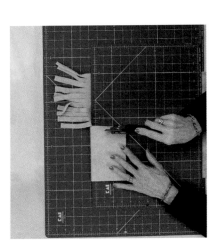

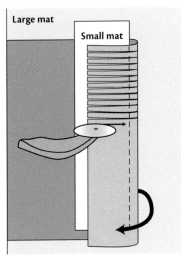

Large mat

Small mat

4. Beginning at the raw edge of the fleece on the smaller mat, rotary cut the fringe by running the cutter onto the larger mat.

Quick fringe can be done on one edge (bottom of a vest), two edges (opposite ends of a scarf, blanket, or pillow), four edges (all sides of a blanket or pillow), a single layer or double layer.

Nancy's Comment

I love the speed of this technique. It is so-o-o much easier than drawing and following cutting lines or (heaven forbid) cutting with scissors.

I am often asked (invariably by quilters whose projects require precision cutting) how I know that each cut is exactly ½" (or ¾" or 1"). When I say, "It doesn't matter. Close counts," half the quilters smile with a newfound freedom while the other half frowns with disapproval.

Much of my love affair with fleece is due to the fact that "close counts." If, however, precision is of prime importance to you, and your stomach would get upset at the "close counts" level of tolerance, use the June Tailor Shape Cut or Shape Cut Plus to cut your fringe precisely. It's all about your comfort zone and tolerance level.

Quick Fringe Idea Gallery

Single-Layer Scarf

MATERIALS

Fleece: ¼ or ⅓ yard

DIRECTIONS

1. Cut the fleece to 9" x 60" or 12" x 60".

2. Follow the basic quick fringe directions (page 93) to cut fringe ½" to ¾" wide and 3" to 5" long.

Optional: Use a specialty rotary blade to make the fringe cuts.

Double-Layer Scarf

Refer to page 62 for step-by-step directions.

MATERIALS

Fleece color #1: ¼ or ⅓ yard

Fleece color #2: ¼ or ⅓ yard

DIRECTIONS

1. Cut two coordinate pieces of fleece 9" x 60" or 12" x 60".

2. Place the fleece layers *wrong* sides together.

3. Pin each short end of the scarf to designate the end of the fringe cuts (3" to 5" from the end of the scarf, depending on how long you want the fringe to be).

4. Using a ½" seam allowance, sew the scarf layers together at both long sides, beginning and ending at the pin marks. (You can sew across the short ends of the scarf, from pin to pin if desired, but it's not necessary.)

5. Using a rotary cutter, trim the scarf close to the seamline, extending the cut all the way to both ends of the scarf.

6. Follow the basic quick fringe directions (page 93) to make fringe cuts ½" to ¾" wide and 3" to 5" long.

Single-Layer Blanket – Quick Fringed on Two Sides

DIRECTIONS

1. Cut the fleece to the desired size.

2. Following the basic quick fringe directions on page 93, cut fringe ½" to ¾" wide and 3" to 5" long on two opposing sides of the blanket.

MATERIALS

Throw (54" x 60"): 1½ yards fleece

Blanket (60" x 72"): 2 yards fleece

Or 1 pre-printed fleece blanket panel

Nancy's Note

When only two sides of a blanket are being fringed, generally the fringe is on the shorter sides. However, you can fringe any two opposing sides if your print dictates otherwise. If you can't decide, quick fringe all four sides! Read on.

Single-Layer Blanket –
Quick Fringed on Four Sides

DIRECTIONS

1. Cut the fleece to the desired size.

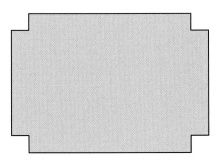

2. Cut away all four corners of the blanket, cutting away squares equal to the fringe length. (Trim away a 3" corner square for 3" fringe, a 4" corner square for 4" fringe, etc.)

3. Following the basic quick fringe directions on page 93, cut fringe ½" to ¾" wide on all four sides of the blanket.

MATERIALS

Throw (54" x 60"): 1½ yards fleece

Blanket (60" x 72"): 2 yards fleece

Or 1 pre-printed fleece blanket panel

Nancy's Comment

Cutting away the four corners eliminates the problem of how to "get around the corner" when fringing. Fringing around the corner would result in uneven skinny cuts fanning to larger edges.

Double-Layer Blanket – Quick Fringed on Two Sides

MATERIALS

Throw (54" x 60"): 1½ yards fleece for each layer

Blanket (60" x 72"): 2 yards fleece for each layer

DIRECTIONS

1. Cut two coordinate pieces of fleece to the desired size.

2. Place the fleece layers *wrong* sides together and pin to secure.

3. Place pins at each "to be fringed" side of the blanket to designate the end of the fringe cuts (3" to 5" from the end of the blanket, depending on how long you want the fringe to be).

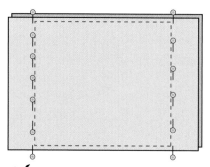

4. Sew the blanket layers together on the long sides, using a ½" seam allowance. Pivot at the pin marks to sew across the sides to be fringed.

5. Using a rotary cutter, trim the blanket close to the long unfringed seamline, extending the cut all the way to both ends of the blanket.

6. Retrue the ends to be fringed if necessary.

7. Following the basic quick fringe directions on page 93, make fringe cuts the desired width, using the stitching line as a guide for the fringe depth. Fringe both layers at once.

8. Refer to page 45 for reverse appliqué directions.

Double-Layer Blanket –
Quick Fringed on Four Sides

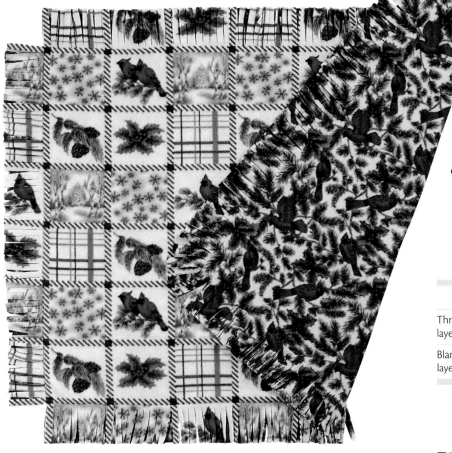

Removing the corners eliminates the dilemma of how to "fringe around the corner."

MATERIALS

Throw (54" x 60"): 1½ yards fleece for each layer

Blanket (60" x 72"): 2 yards fleece for each layer

DIRECTIONS

1. Cut the two fleeces to the desired size.

2. Arrange the fleece layers with wrong sides together.

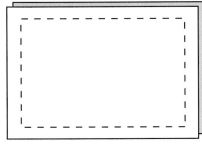

3. Sew the fleece layers together using a 3" to 5" seam allowance (whatever depth you want the fringe to be).

Nancy's Hint
If you have a quilt bar accessory for your machine, use it as a stitching guide for the seamlines. (A quilt bar is not just for quilting.)

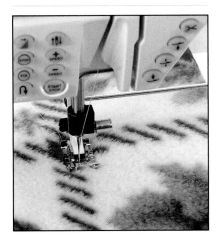

4. Cut out all four corners, cutting away squares equal to the fringe length. (Trim away 3" square corners for 3" fringe, 4" corners for 4" fringe, etc.)

5. Following the basic quick fringe directions on page 93, make fringe cuts the desired width on all four sides of the blanket, fringing both layers at once. Use the stitching line as a guide for the fringe depth.

No-Sew Blanket

This is a fun alternative to sewing. (And a perfect project to make during a power outage. Cut and tie by candlelight!) It's also a great take-along project to keep hands busy during long road trips.

MATERIALS

Main fleece: 1½ yards

Contrast fleece: 1½ yards

No-Sew Guidelines

- Begin with two square cuts of fleece.
- Cut blanket layers 3" larger on all sides (6" total dimension) than the desired finished blanket. For example:
  - 60" x 60" beginning fleece size yields a 54" x 54" finished blanket
  - 54" x 54" beginning fleece size yields a 48" x 48" finished blanket

  The baby blanket shown is 45" x 45" (finished), so both layers were initially cut 51" x 51", which is 6" larger all around.

DIRECTIONS

1. Cut both fleece layers to size (6" larger than the desired finished size).

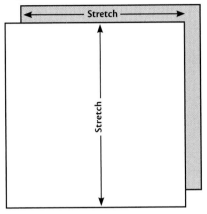

2. Place the fleece layers *wrong* sides together (finished position), offsetting the direction of most stretch in the layers.

3. Cut out 3" squares from all four corners (the length of the fringe).

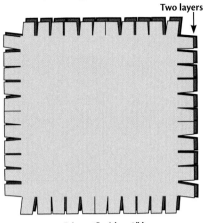

Fringe 1" wide x 3" long

4. Following the basic quick fringe directions on page 93, fringe both layers at once. Make the fringe cuts 1" wide x 3" long.

Nancy's Note

*Offsetting stretch factors **only apply to** **no-sew** projects. In other double-layer fringe projects there's no need to address the direction of stretch because it doesn't affect the technique or the end use. However, when making a no-sew project, the layers are arranged so that the greater degree of stretch on each layer is opposite the other layer. Because fleece is stretchy in one direction and quite stable in the other, offsetting the stretches gives one stretchy fringe cut and one stable fringe cut in each knot. (Two "stretchies" are hard to work with and two "stable fringe cuts" lay flat.)*

5. Tie each fringe pair (upper and under layer) into a square knot. Snug each knot close to the blanket base to avoid large gaps between the knots.

Nancy's Comment

The beauty of quick fringing both layers together is that you automatically have matching fringe pairs to tie into knots.

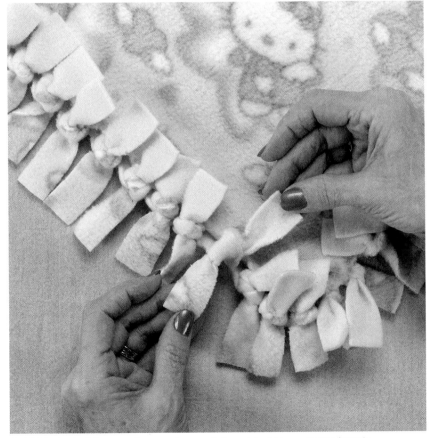

Quick fringing both layers at the same time results in matched fringe pairs ready to tie.

No-Sew Pillow

This pillow is an easy-to-make project for nonsewers. The flavor changes dramatically depending on the pillow size and fleece combinations you choose. Smaller pillows in little-girl colors of pink and blue are perfect for a feminine bedroom. Large pillows in earth tones make great den floor pillows. Large pillows made in school colors, with longer ties and perhaps school letters or a sports appliqué make great team spirit builders.

MATERIALS

Square pillow form

2 fleece layers 6" larger than pillow form

DIRECTIONS

1. Cut the pillow front and back 3" larger on all sides (6" total) than the desired finished pillow size. If you have a 16" pillow form, cut the fleece 22" x 22". For a 14" pillow form, cut the fleece 20" x 20".

2. Place the fleece layers with *wrong* sides together, offsetting the direction of the most stretch in the layers.

3. Following the directions for the no-sew blanket on page 101, quick fringe the pillow layers and tie the fringes together on three sides.

4. Insert the pillow form and tie the fourth side.

Simple Rag Quilt

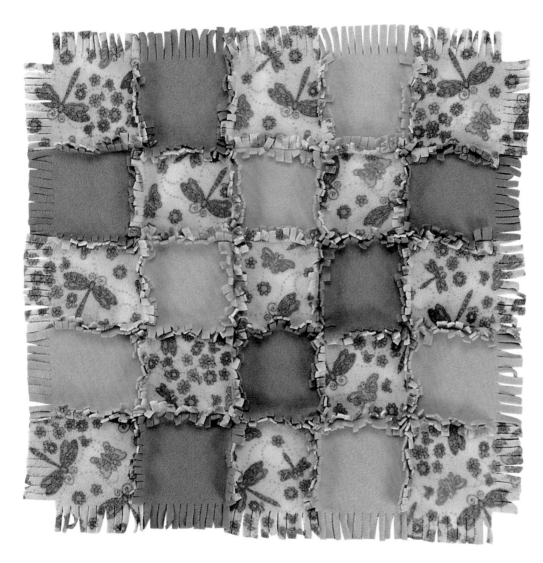

The quick-fringe-before-you-sew method is much easier than the scissor-clip-after-you-sew method.

The first question I am always asked when showing a rag quilt is, "What size are the squares?" When I say that it doesn't matter, traditional quilters frown at me with strong disapproval, generally muttering, "You'll never be a quilter."

But it *really* doesn't matter. They are all squares and there is no piecing involved so they can be any size you want as long as they are *all the same* size. Cut the squares 2" larger than the desired finished square size to account for the 1" fringe cuts.

The quilt featured here is small. The 30" x 30" finished size uses smaller squares (pint-sized to coordinate with the little girl robe on page 83). See page 104 for suggested dimensions and yardage to convert this to an adult-sized version.

The rag quilt directions given here are simple and straightforward. They use 1" fringe around all the squares and for the blanket perimeter. You could make the fringe 1½" long for a shaggier look. Or you could make the perimeter fringe longer than the interior fringe. The options are many. Decide before you start and cut the squares accordingly.

As introduced in *Polar Magic*, the fleece rag quilt can be made in a variety of ways: single layer using one, two, three, or more prints and solids; single layer with a blunt edge appliqué; or double layer with reverse appliqué.

Whether you are making it single or double layer, the construction is the same. If you want blunt edge appliqué or reverse appliqué on some of the squares, do the appliqué work before constructing the blanket.

MATERIALS

Print fleece: ½ yard

Solid color #1 (purple): ¼ yard

Solid color #2 (turquoise): ¼ yard

P	1	P	2	P
1	P	2	P	1
P	2	P	1	P
2	P	1	P	2
P	1	P	2	P

Layout Key
P = print　　　　1 = color #1　　　2 = color #2

Large Rag Quilt

To adapt the simple rag quilt to a larger size (51" x 65"), use the same directions with the following changes.

MATERIALS

Print fleece: 1½ yards

Solid color #1 (purple): ¾ yard

Solid color #2 (turquoise): ¾ yard

DIRECTIONS

1. Cut the following:
- Print fleece
    32 squares 9" x 9"
- Solid color #1
    16 squares 9" x 9"
- Solid color #2
    15 squares 9" x 9"

2. The layout is the same except that instead of being 5 squares wide x 5 squares long, the larger blanket is 7 squares wide x 9 squares long. Lengthen the top row sequence (P-1-P-2-P-1-P), continuing the sequence as you spill over into the next row.

DIRECTIONS

1. Cut the fleece as follows:
- Print fleece
    13 squares 8" x 8"
- Fleece color #1
    6 squares 8" x 8"
- Fleece color #2
    6 squares 8" x 8"

2. Cut out 1" corner squares from all the fleece squares.

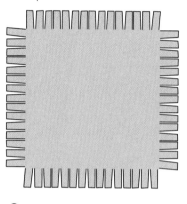

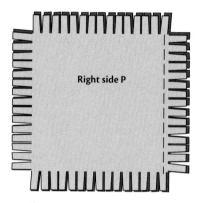

△3. Quick fringe all sides of all the squares. Make the fringe cuts ½" wide and 1" long. (Refer to page 93 for directions.)

△4. With *wrong* sides together, place a print (P) square on top of a color #1 (1) square. Sew the squares together along the right edge, sewing from corner cutout to corner cutout. Be careful not to catch any fringe in the seamline.

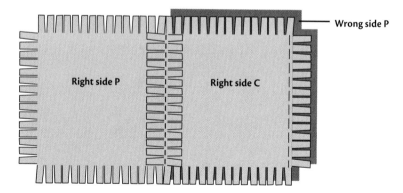

△5. With *wrong* sides together, place the just sewn P/1 pair on top of the next P square. Sew the squares together along the right edge, sewing from corner cutout to corner cutout.

6. Refer to the layout diagram and continue adding squares to finish the top row.

7. Refer to the layout diagram and sew the second through the fifth rows.

8. With *wrong* sides together, pin and stitch the top row to the second row, matching the seamlines. Be careful not to catch any fringe in the stitching.

9. Sew the remaining rows together to complete the quilt.

Bunny Ears Baby Blanket

The bunny ears edge finish is a clever and charming quick fringe edge finish that looks like bunny ears on the right side and twisted braid on the wrong side. The key to successful bunny ears is a tiny slit. Read on and you'll see what I mean. The dimensions can vary. The fringe can be cut longer and wider for slightly different effects. (Longer fringe may result in a flop-eared bunny!) Experiment on a scrap of fleece first.

MATERIALS

Fleece yardage sufficient to make blanket size desired

36" x 36" or 36" x 45":	1 yard
45" x 45" or 45" x 60":	1¼ yards

Note: *Take into account that 4" will be used to make the bunny ears.*

DIRECTIONS

1. Cut a baby blanket to the desired size.

2. Cut out 2" squares from all four of the blanket corners.

3. Quick fringe the blanket edges, cutting the fringe 1¼" wide x 2" long. (Refer to page 93 for directions.)

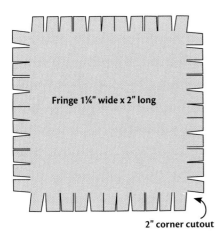

Fringe 1¼" wide x 2" long

2" corner cutout

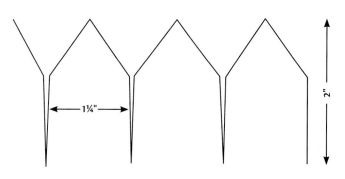

△4. Cut the ends of each fringe cut into a point. I call this "picket fencing." Don't bother to measure – just cut the fringe ends into points. If one point looks a little lopsided, simply recut it.

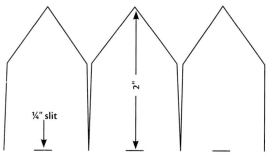

△5. Using a small (18mm) rotary cutter, make a *tiny* slit at the bottom center of each fringe cut. (The slit must be tiny, just a nick, maybe ¼" wide. Very narrow, so that when the fringe is fed through the slit, the slit pinches the fleece, puckering it to form a bunny ear.)

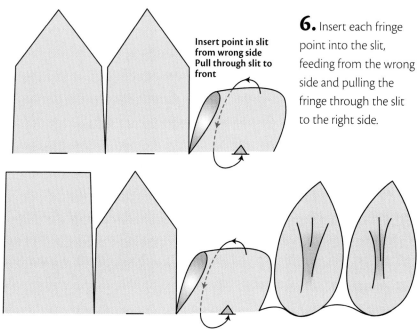

Insert point in slit from wrong side Pull through slit to front

6. Insert each fringe point into the slit, feeding from the wrong side and pulling the fringe through the slit to the right side.

This charming fringe variation turns ordinary fringe into "bunny ears."

Nancy's Hint

An easy way to pull the picket-fenced fringe through the tiny slit is to insert the tips of narrow serger tweezers through the slit, pinch the fringe tip, and pull it through.

Boa

A boa is a fun way to use up leftover fleece pieces and add spice to a plain winter jacket at the same time. (If you participate in gift exchanges, this would be a fun item to share. Definitely an attention-getter!) Mix and match prints and/or solids.

MATERIALS

Two-color boa

 color #1: ⅓ yard

 color #2: ⅓ yard

Four-color boa

 4 different colors, each 6" x 60"

Size 16/100 universal sewing machine needle

DIRECTIONS

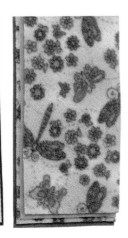

1. Cut four 6" x 60" layers.

2. Stack the fleece layers as desired, alternating the colors, all with right sides facing up.

3. Sew a 4mm wide x 4mm long zigzag stitch down the center of the stacked strips, backtacking at the beginning and ending to secure the stitches.

4. Fringe the layers, cutting ½" wide fringes through four layers at a time.

Nancy's Hint

It's too bulky to quick fringe. Just rotary cut the fringe, cutting four layers at once.

5. Shake the fringed boa to fluff the cuts.

Curly Boa

A variation of the boa, this one requires that you cut the length of the fleece pieces on the lengthwise straight-of-grain so that the fringe cuts are made in the direction of most stretch. (The fringe cuts need to be stretchy so they will curl.)

Since the fringe is going to be stretched and curled, it really doesn't matter whether the fleece right or wrong sides are facing up during construction.

MATERIALS

Fleece color #1 (royal): ⅝ yard

Fleece color #2 (white): ⅝ yard

Size 16/100 universal sewing machine needle

DIRECTIONS

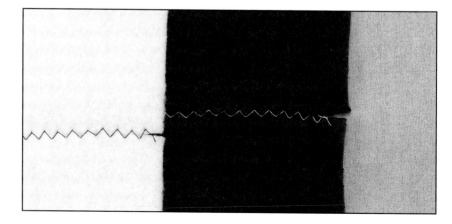

1. Cut color #1 fleece into three 13" x 22½" pieces . (It's important that the greater stretch is in the 13" direction.)

2. Cut color #2 fleece into three 12" x 22½" pieces . (It's important that the greater stretch is in the 12" direction.)

3. Abut the ends and stitch together the three color #1 pieces to make one 13" x 67½" long piece. Use a 4mm wide x 4mm long zigzag stitch.

4. Abut the ends and stitch together the three color #2 pieces to make one 12" x 67½" long piece. Use a 4mm wide x 4mm long zigzag stitch.

5. Draw a centerline down the length of color #2 (white).

6. Lay the long color #2 (white) piece on top of the long color #1 (royal) piece (½" of color #1 will extend on both sides).

7. Fold one double-layer side over onto itself, bringing the raw edges to the drawn centerline. (Having color #1 narrower than color #2 reduces the bulk and allows you to bring both edges together at the center.)

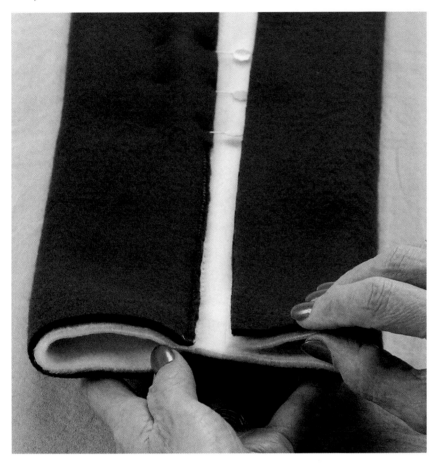

8. Sew a 4mm wide x 4mm long zigzag stitch, securing the cut edges to the center of the boa. (You are sewing through four layers: the center two layers and the folded-over raw edge two layers.)

9. Fold the other double-layer side over onto itself, meeting the raw edges at the centerline.

10. Zigzag stitch to secure the cut edges to the center.

11. Cut the folded-over layers into ¼" to ⅜" fringe. (You will actually be fringing four layers at a time.) Cut the fringe as close to the center stitching lines as possible without cutting the stitches. It is too bulky to quick fringe. Just rotary cut the fringe, cutting four layers at one time.

12. Pinch each individual fringe loop and quickly stretch and release to form a curly looped fleece yarn.

Nancy's Hint

Curling the fringed fleece loops is a lot like raking scissors over curling ribbon to curl it. It is a quick motion rather than a slow and deliberate process. If it doesn't curl quite well enough the first time, stretch it again.

13. Shake the boa to separate the loops and to fluff. Toss it in a no-heat dryer to remove the fleece lint. The loops will fall more to one side of the boa, essentially creating a front and back.

Beaded Vest and Scarf

Use your favorite vest pattern as is or convert it into a no-side-seam garment. Refer to page 122 for directions on changing a garment to no-side-seam.

MATERIALS

Vest: 1 yard fleece

Scarf: ¼ yard fleece

6mm x 9mm pony beads

Fasturn tube turner or size US9/1.25mm metal crochet hook (to apply beads)

BEADING DIRECTIONS

1. Stack the pony beads on the metal pigtail Fasturn hook or a metal crochet hook.

2. Hook a fringed end and slide a bead onto the fringe.

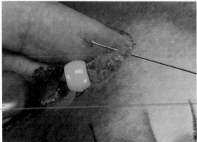

3. Tie a single knot at the fringe end and slide the bead down to the knot.

Nancy's Hint

For an interesting effect, vary the number of beads on the fringe cuts. This vest features a 1-2-3-2-1-2-3-2 bead sequence.

Nancy's Caution

Don't use beaded fringe on items for babies or toddlers. The beads could be pulled off and swallowed.

VEST DIRECTIONS

1. Cut out the vest according to the directions on your pattern or convert it to a no-side-seam garment by following the directions on page 122.

2. Quick fringe the lower edge of the vest with cuts ½" wide x 5" long. (The extra length is for the beads and knots.)

Nancy's Note

If the vest has a pointed front lower edge, do not quick fringe. It's difficult to accurately quick fringe pointed areas.

3. Sew the side seams (if applicable) and the shoulder seams using the seam allowance given in your pattern.

4. Turn under ½" at the armhole edges and topstitch to secure.

5. Turn under ½" at the center front and neck edges. Topstitch to secure.

SCARF DIRECTIONS

1. Cut the scarf to 9" x 60".

2. Fringe each short end with cuts ½" wide x 5" long.

3. Place beads on each fringe as desired, knotting the ends to secure.

Nancy's Note

You could also bead fringe the lower edge of a bolero style jacket, tunic vest, pullover, or poncho.

I admit that newer and quicker isn't always easier. When I designed this pointed scarf to be part of a scarf collection pattern #4263 for McCall Pattern Co., I found it easier and more accurate to fringe the "old-fashioned" way – laying the scarf flat and using a ruler and rotary cutter. It was difficult to maintain the correct angle on the pointed ends and keep the cuts parallel when using the quick fringe technique.

Chapter 7

Putting the Techniques to Use

This chapter will show you how to incorporate a variety of fleece techniques and ideas into your everyday sewing. You'll learn how to take advantage of fleece's unique characteristics and combine innovative techniques for ease of construction, speedy sewing, and effective results.

SCARF DIRECTIONS

1. Use a decorative blade rotary cutter to cut the scarf 9" x 60", gently rounding the corners.

2. From the contrast (red) fleece, cut six 4½" square appliqué patches.

3. Transfer the flower template to the right side of three of the patches, using mesh transfer canvas and a water-soluble pencil. (Refer to page 18 for design transferring directions.)

4. Sandwich the scarf between a traced appliqué patch and a plain appliqué patch at the desired motif placement. Hold the patches in place by lightly spraying temporary adhesive on the wrong sides of the patches (in the centers) or by pinning. (Refer to page 44 for double-sided appliqué directions.)

5. Stitch the flower outline through all three layers.

6. Trim the excess contrast fleece (patches) close to the stitching lines, resulting in a double-sided appliqué.

7. Repeat for the other two sets of flower appliqués, randomly arranging them on the scarf.

SCARF MATERIALS

Fleece main color (white): ¼ yard

Fleece contrast color (red): ⅛ yard

Decorative blade rotary cutter

Crusher Hat/Scarf Flower template on page 153

The perfectly matched double-sided appliqué looks like it required tedious precision work but it's lots of fun and very easy.

Fleece Chenille Baby Blanket

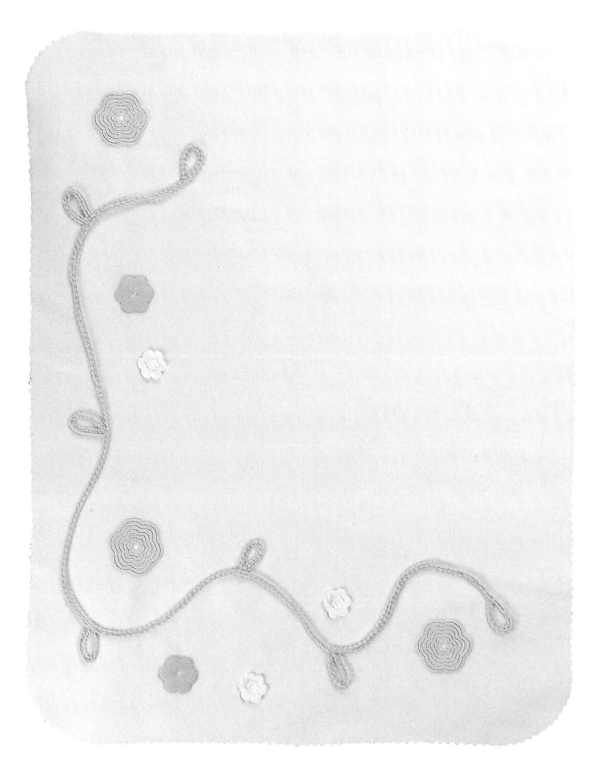

Here's another project that incorporates lots of techniques — chenille embellishment, chenille strips, blunt edge appliqué, dimensional blunt edge appliqué, and blunt edge finish.

DIRECTIONS

1. Using a wave blade rotary cutter, cut the main color (white) fleece to 36" x 45", gently rounding the corners.

2. From pink fleece, cut three 4½" squares (for the chenille posies).

3. From blue fleece, cut two 4½" squares (for the blunt edge appliqué posies).

4. From yellow fleece, cut three 4½" squares (for the dimensional posies).

5. With the pinking blade rotary cutter, cut four ½" x 60" strips of mint fleece (for the chenille strip stem and leaves). Refer to page 76 to make two mint chenille strips for the stem and leaves.

6. Place wash-away basting tape on the back (flat) side of one mint chenille strip for the stem. Place a pin 6" from one end of the chenille stem (this 6" will be used later to create a leaf).

7. Place the blanket right side up on a table. Referring to the photo for placement, arrange the mint chenille stem, beginning with the pin mark, in a gently waved line along two sides of the blanket. Allow 6" at the end of the mint chenille stem for another leaf. (You may have more than 6" left, depending on how wavy you made the stem.)

8. *Don't tape* the stem in place yet – pin it instead. This is just a general placement so you can arrange the posy motifs.

9. Using the posy templates on page 152, draw and cut out paper templates (three large, two medium, three small). Arrange the paper posies along the pinned mint chenille stem. (Refer to the photo for placement.) Pin the paper posies on the blanket and use as placement guide for the posy appliqués.

MATERIALS

Fleece main color (white): 1 yard

Fleece contrast (pink, blue, yellow, mint): ⅛ each

Rotary cutters: wave blade and pinking blade

Wash-away basting tape

8 white size 20 sport snaps or ⅜" white buttons or machine-stitched dots for posy centers

Small, Medium, and Large Posy templates on page 152

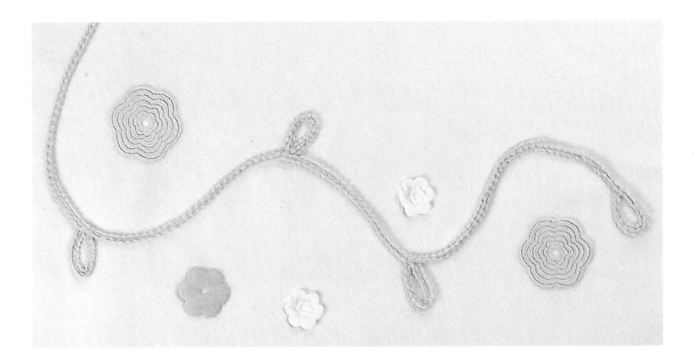

PINK CHENILLE POSY APPLIQUÉS

1. Using mesh transfer canvas and a water-soluble pencil, draw the large posy motif on the right side of the three pink fleece squares (see page 18).

2. Pin the pink squares on the blanket and stitch the posy outline.

3. Stitch a second row, inside and ¼" away from the outline stitching.

4. Repeat, stitching a total of five or six rows.

5. Using appliqué scissors, trim the excess pink fleece from the posy appliqué.

6. Use the points of the appliqué scissors to carefully cut open the stitching channels.

BLUE BLUNT EDGE POSY APPLIQUÉS

1. Using mesh transfer canvas and a water-soluble pencil, draw the medium posy motif on the right side of the two blue fleece squares (see page 18).

2. Pin the blue squares on the blanket.

3. Stitch the posy outline.

4. Using appliqué scissors, trim the excess blue fleece from the posy appliqué.

YELLOW DIMENSIONAL BLUNT EDGE POSY APPLIQUÉS

1. Using mesh transfer canvas and a water-soluble pencil, draw the small posy motif on the right side of the three yellow fleece squares (see page 18).

2. Cut out the yellow posies. Mark the right side with a pin.

3. Pin the yellow posies in place on the blanket.

4. Stitch the yellow posies to the blanket by topstitching ⅜" to ½" away from the outer edge of the flower.

POSY CENTERS

1. Attach a white sport snap, white button, or machine satin stitch a white round dot for the posy centers.

STEM AND LEAVES

1. Remove the protective paper from the basting tape and adhere the mint chenille stem to the blanket.

2. To make a leaf at the beginning, loop the cut end of the stem to the 6" pin mark, tucking the cut end under the stem, and adhere it to the blanket.

3. Continue adhering the stem to the blanket, forming a soft wavy line. Lift and rearrange as necessary.

4. Form a leaf at the end of the stem by looping the cut end back to meet the 6" pin mark. Tuck the cut end under the stem and adhere.

5. For the remaining leaves, adhere basting tape to the wrong side of 30" of the remaining stem piece and cut five 6" pieces.

6. Form loops to create leaves and arrange them along the stem, tucking the cut ends under the stem. Adhere them in place.

7. Stitch the stem to the blanket by sewing down the middle of the stem and around the leaves as you come to them. Use a 4mm long straight stitch.

Nancy's Hint

Choose a presser foot that has a bar between the presser foot toes in front of the needle. The bar will help to keep the chenille strip uncurled as the needle stitches the stem in place. Use the flat prong of the stiletto to guide the chenille stem under the presser foot.

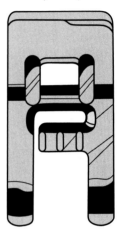

Attention Embroidery Machine Owners

If you have the book, Embroidery Machine Essentials: Fleece Techniques, you can stitch the flowers on your embroidery machine. Use the entire Nested Flower motif for the chenille appliqué (pink flower); stitch segments 5, 8, and 9 for the blunt edge appliqué (blue flower); use the small posy paper template to cut out three yellow posies. Attach dimensional posy appliqués by stitching segments 2, 8, and 9.

Crystal Snowflake Scarf

Generally speaking, heat-set embellishment techniques are not appropriate for fleece. The necessary heat and pressure tend to damage the fleece surface. However, the L'Orna Decorative Touch hot fix applicator wand has opened the door for successfully applying heat-set crystals and nail heads on fleece.

If you can't find the L'Orna Decorative Touch hot fix applicator wand and high quality stones or nail head embellishments at your local fabric or craft retailer, refer to the Resources on page 150.

MATERIALS

¼ yard fleece

L'Orna Decorative Touch hot fix applicator wand (with interchangeable tips)

Swarovski heat-set Austrian crystals

Nail head embellishments

Straight or wave rotary blade

Crystal Snowflake template on page 154

Nancy's Comment

I've seen a lot of heat-fix crystals and stones. The Swarovski brand is the prettiest and affix the most permanently.

DIRECTIONS

1. Cut the scarf 9" x 60".

2. If using a straight blade, fringe the scarf ends by cutting fringe ½" wide x 4" long. If using a decorative edge blade, shape the scarf ends as desired.

3. Use mesh transfer canvas and a water-soluble pencil to trace the Crystal Snowflake template lines on the right side of the fleece (see page 18).

4. Following the manufacturer's directions, attach the appropriate tip and heat the hot fix applicator to temperature.

5. Following the manufacturer's directions, adhere miscellaneous stones and nail heads to the traced Crystal Snowflake template. (Refer to the photo for placement.)

Nancy's Note

Under normal circumstances, this "pick up the stone and set it to adhere" procedure is adequate. However, adhering embellishments to a fuzzy napped surface can cause problems. To ensure a solid bond, after setting the stone use a small tool (screwdriver tip or serger tweezers tip) to push down on the hot stone to solidly imbed it in the fleece.

No-Side-Seam Chenille Vest

The no-side-seam vest was introduced in my first book, **Adventures With Polarfleece®**, as an easy way to eliminate side seams on fleece garments, either to preserve a print or to reduce bulk. This approach works well for both vests and jackets.

When choosing a commercial pattern to change into a no-side-seam design, it is necessary to find a pattern with simple fronts (plain right and left front with no darts or additional seams), a one-piece back, and relatively straight side seams. If the pattern includes side seam pockets, eliminate them.

Here I show a vest but the same approach applies to a jacket. In jacket construction, the sleeve would be sewn, then set into the jacket armhole. (This may be a minor change from the order of construction in the pattern directions.)

MATERIALS

Fleece print: 1⅜ to 1⅝ yards. Calculate the garment body length + ⅜ (to make chenille yardage) + ¼ yard (for fat piping)

Fleece solid: 1⅛ to 1⅜ yards (for chenille under layer)

Nancy's Note

The main body yardage requirements may seem overly generous. When making such a large piece of chenille yardage, there will be some shifting of layers as well as angling of the channels. The generous yardage gives extra room to lay out the garment accordingly.

CONVERTING A PATTERN TO NO SIDE SEAMS

1. Overlap the front and back pattern pieces at the underarm points, overlapping twice the seam allowance depth. Overlap 1¼" if the pattern calls for ⅝" seam allowances. Overlap ½" if the pattern calls for ¼" seam allowances.

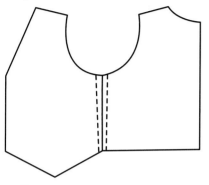

▲2. Adjust the amount of overlap at the bottom edge of the garment so that the center back fold line is parallel to the front straight-of-grain line.

Nancy's Note
The overlap may be less at the bottom edge than at the underarm point, but that's okay. It's more important to maintain straight-of-grain than a consistent overlap.

3. Pin, tape, or stitch the pattern pieces together to create one pattern piece.

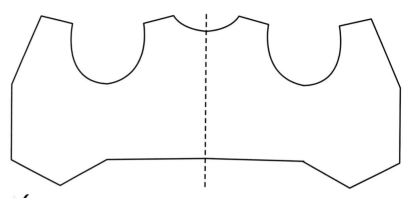

▲4. Cut out the fronts and back as one fabric piece (front, back on fold, front).

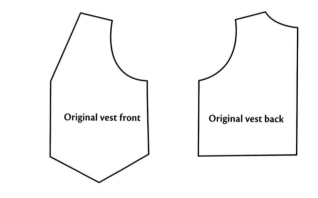

Original vest front   Original vest back

NO-SIDE-SEAM CHENILLE VEST DIRECTIONS

1. From the fleece print, cut three 3" x 60" strips for the fat piping trim. Cut on the crossgrain (direction of most stretch).

2. With both right sides facing up, lay the print yardage on top of the solid yardage and pin the layers together.

3. Make the chenille yardage. (Refer to page 76 for chenille yardage directions.)

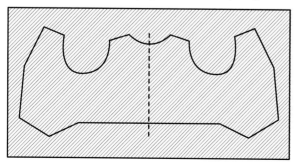

▲4. Cut out the garment, taking care that the chenille angles at both center fronts are complementary to each other.

Nancy's Hint
I found it easier to see my chenille stitching lines when stitching on the solid fleece. I first drew a rough outline of the vest, drew angled guidelines, stitched rows, then cut out the garment.

Nancy's Note
Stitching so many rows on a lofted stretch fabric is not an exact science. Even though you stitch carefully, the lines tend to shift and change a little. Before cutting, gently manipulate the fabric as necessary to make the chenille lines at the center front edges have the same angle. (It sure is nice that fleece is so forgiving and easy to work with.)

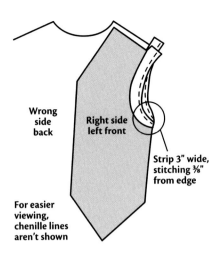

Wrong side back

Right side left front

Strip 3" wide, stitching ⅜" from edge

For easier viewing, chenille lines aren't shown

▲**5.** With right sides together, place a fleece trim strip against the *left* armhole and stitch with an exact ⅜" seam allowance.

Nancy's Note

Right and left refer to the garment as when you're wearing it.

6. Finger press the trim strip away from the garment (toward the armhole opening).

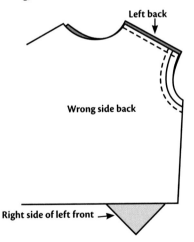

Left back

Wrong side back

Right side of left front

▲**7.** Sew the *left* shoulder seam (from the neck edge through the unfinished edge of the trim). Refer to your pattern directions for the seam allowance depth.

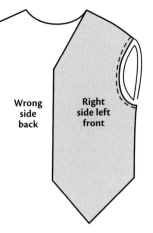

Wrong side back

Right side left front

▲**8.** Wrap the trim strip up, around, and over the raw edges, encasing both seam allowances, and pin it in place. Stitch in the ditch to secure.

9. Trim and remove the excess trim strip close to the stitching. (Refer to page 65 for directions.)

10. Repeat for the *right* armhole using the remaining trim strip. *Do not sew the shoulder seam or finish the trim at this time.*

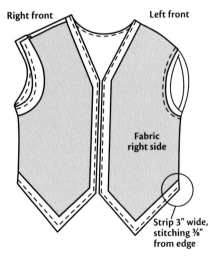

Right front   **Left front**

Fabric right side

Strip 3" wide, stitching ⅜" from edge

▲**11.** With right sides together, and beginning at the neck edge of the unsewn right shoulder seam, sew a trim strip to the right vest front, across the right front lower edge, around the back, across the left front lower edge, up the left front, around the back neck edge, and end at the unsewn right shoulder edge. (Refer to page 69 for splicing directions.)

12. Finger press the fleece trim away from the garment.

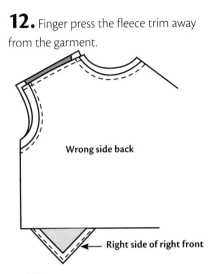

Wrong side back

Right side of right front

▲**13.** Sew the right shoulder seam. Sew from the outermost unfinished edge of the trim at the armhole, through the garment shoulder to the end on the unfinished edge of the trim at the neck edge. Refer to your pattern directions for the seam allowance depth.

14. Wrap, pin, stitch in the ditch, and trim the excess strip to finish the right armhole. (Refer to page 65 for directions.)

15. Wrap, pin, stitch, and trim the excess strip to finish the complete vest outer edge.

Patchwork Embroidered Quilt

The goal for this lovely blanket is to make the wrong side look as pretty as the right side. Using decorative threads in both the needle and bobbin, water-soluble stabilizer, and lapped seamlines makes the blanket pretty on both sides.

The embroidery designs shown are from my book, *Embroidery Machine Essentials: Fleece Techniques*. You can use any embroidery machine designs you like.

DIRECTIONS

1. Use a straight rotary blade to cut the following 9" x 9" squares:

- 9 from color #1 (blue)
- 8 from color #2 (pink)
- 8 from color #3 (green)

Nancy's Comment

The beginning square size is a little larger than you actually need. This extra allows you to trim and perfectly center each embroidered motif. (I find it easier to "trim to center" than embroider exactly in the center.)

2. Hoop the heavyweight water-soluble stabilizer and lightly mist it to make it tacky.

3. With the right side facing up, adhere a fleece square to the damp stabilizer.

4. Center the embroidery design in the stitching area.

MATERIALS

Note: This will yield a finished quilt size of 40" x 40"

Fleece color #1 (blue): ½ yard

Fleece color #2 (pink): ½ yard

Fleece color #3 (green): ½ yard

Straight and wave blade rotary cutter

Wash-away double-sided basting tape

3 open work embroidery designs

Rayon thread to complement fleece colors

Construction thread – one color to blend with all fleece colors

Sulky Ultra Solvy (or similar) heavyweight water-soluble stabilizer

5. With matching rayon thread in the needle and bobbin, stitch the design in the center of the fleece square.

6. Remove the fleece and stabilizer from the hoop and trim away as much stabilizer as possible.

7. Embroider a total of five color #1 (blue) squares, four color #2 (pink) squares, and four color #3 (green) squares.

8. Refer to the manufacturer's directions and soak the embroidery squares to dissolve the stabilizer.

9. Use a wave blade rotary cutter to cut all the squares to 8" x 8", centering the embroidered motifs.

10. Follow the layout illustration to lap, tape, and stitch the squares together. (Refer to the Patchwork Scarf on page 25 for blunt edge lapped seam directions.)

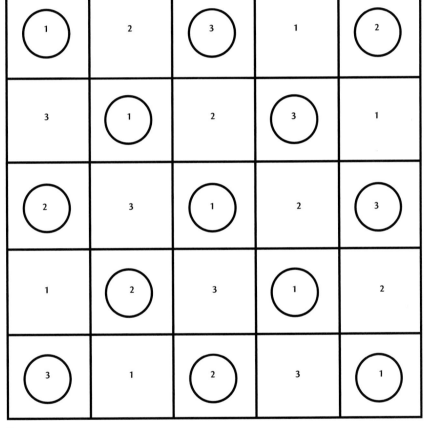

Key
1 = color #1
2 = color #2
3 = color #3
O = embroidered square

Nancy's Note #1

In most lapping projects, I lap left over right. In this blanket, I lapped right over left. It really doesn't make a difference as long as you are consistent throughout the project.

Nancy's Note #2

Since the embroidery motifs I used weren't heavily stitch-filled, there was no need for a topping.

Nancy's Note #3

If you are using the designs from *Embroidery Machine Essentials*, stitch the Crystal Snowflake, all segments, Small Framed Leaf, segments 4, 5, and 10, and Fir Tree, segments 2 and 4.

Quilted Blanket Panel

*Team a preprinted fleece blanket panel with a coordinate solid fleece, outline
stitch the dominant motif, and you get a cozy blanket with a quilt flavor.*

DIRECTIONS

1. Cut the solid fleece for the blanket panel back and sew it to the panel print with wrong sides together and quick fringe the edges. Use the preprinted fringe lines on the panel print as stitching lines. (Refer to page 99 for double-layer quick fringe directions.)

2. If there are no preprinted fringe lines on the panel print and there is no printed border suitable for fringing, choose one of the following edge finishes:

    a. Sew the blanket layers together using a ½" seam allowance. Rotary trim close to the seamline. (Refer to page 30 for blunt edge finish directions.)

    b. Use the cheater's wrapped edge technique and a ½" seam allowance. (Refer to page 68 for directions.)

    c. Use the reverse hem technique #1 or #2 (see page 34 for directions.)

3. Pin the layers together on the print side, pinning randomly.

4. With the print facing up, stitch on the dominant lines of the panel print. The bobbin stitches will create a subtle quilted motif on the solid side (back) of the blanket. If you are proficient at it, consider free-motion stitching the design lines.

Nancy's Stitching Hint

To avoid excessive shifting of layers when stitching the blanket layers together, lengthen the stitch length to 3.5mm. When stitching on the crossgrain (direction of most stretch), lengthen the stitch to 4mm to prevent distortion.

MATERIALS

Fleece blanket panel print

Coordinate solid color fleece: yardage to match panel print (usually 1⅓ yards)

Quilter's Pillow

Fleece and quilting aren't typically combined in the same project, but the quilt block motif framed by chenille in this pillow lends a definite quilt flavor. The directions for these pillows are the same. The only difference is the placement of the chenille accent lines.

DIRECTIONS

1. From the main color (white), cut one pillow front 19" x 19" (3" larger than the pillow form) and cut two pillow half backs, 17½" x 12¾". (If you have enough fleece and nap is not an issue, cut the 17½" with the least degree of stretch.)

2. From the contrast color (pink) cut one pillow front under layer 19" x 19" and cut one fat piping strip 3" x 60".

3. On the right side of the pillow front (white), draw one horizontal and one vertical line, intersecting in the middle.

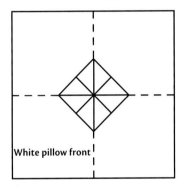

White pillow front

4. Use mesh transfer canvas and a water-soluble pencil to transfer the quilt block template to the center of the pillow front, turning the square to be a diamond.

5. With right sides facing up, place the white pillow front on top of the contrast (pink) fleece. Pin to secure.

6. Stitch the quilt block lines, sewing the fleece layers together.

7. Use appliqué scissors to trim out only the top layer (white) from every other quilt block section, revealing the colored under layer. The result is a pinwheel. (Refer to the photo.)

8. Starting outside one long side of the quilt block (rather than at a corner), straight stitch around the entire quilt block motif, pivoting at the corners, stitching ⅜" away from block outline.

9. Again beginning on one long side of the quilt block, sew a second, third, fourth, and fifth row of stitching, spaced ⅜" apart. You will have five channels to slash open for chenille. (Refer to the photo.)

10. Cut open the channels to create chenille. (Refer to page 75 for chenille directions.)

11. Trim the contrast (pink) fleece under layer close to the outermost chenille stitching line.

12. Trim the pillow front to 17½" x 17½".

13. Refer to the Southwest Pillows on page 137 for directions to finish the pillow.

MATERIALS

Fleece main color (white): ⅝ yard

Fleece contrast color (pink): ⅝ yard (fat piping trim and chenille "peek through")

Quilt Block template on page 155

16" pillow form

Attention Embroidery Machine Owners

If you have my book, Embroidery Machine Essentials: Fleece Techniques, *you can stitch the center motif on your embroidery machine. Simply use the outline stitch, segment 2, from the Pinwheel Block motif.*

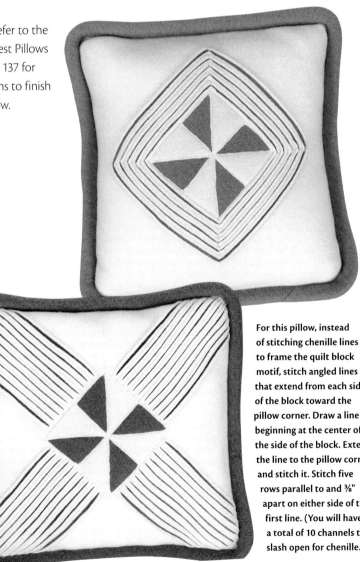

For this pillow, instead of stitching chenille lines to frame the quilt block motif, stitch angled lines that extend from each side of the block toward the pillow corner. Draw a line beginning at the center of the side of the block. Extend the line to the pillow corner and stitch it. Stitch five rows parallel to and ⅜" apart on either side of the first line. (You will have a total of 10 channels to slash open for chenille.)

Scalloped Fleece Yarn

This delightful idea for using fleece yarn was graciously offered to me by Gail Kellogg, a Husqvarna Viking Educator. Gail and my paths have crossed many times at seminars, shows, and conventions around the country and I love her refreshing approach to sewing. She designed this little doll outfit and technique for a special event where she taught the class, "Sewing for Your Ginny Doll."

DIRECTIONS

1. Construct the garment or blanket you've chosen.

2. Make enough fleece yarn to cover the edges you desire. (Refer to page 48 for directions.)

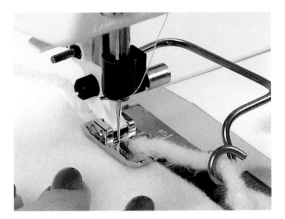

3. Place the fleece yarn under the presser foot, abutting it to the raw edge of the garment or blanket you wish to edge finish. Choose a wide (4mm to 6mm) multiple step stitch to join the fleece yarn to the edge.

Don't stop yet…Now's the time to play a little. Change the thickness of the yarn (begin with a ½" strip of fleece) or experiment with various multi-step stitches (honeycomb, ladder stitch, feather stitch, overlock, blindhem, etc.) and you'll find a lovely assortment of scalloped and decorative edges.

Nancy's Note

Gail said she used this same technique 25 years ago on an Easter dress for her daughter. Back then she used buttonhole twist thread for the decorative scallop edge finish. It's amazing what happens when you add new tricks to old techniques!

MATERIALS

Fleece yardage for garment or blanket (for doll or baby)

⅛ yard contrast fleece for making fleece yarn

Nancy's Comment

Specialized presser feet and machine accessories simplify many procedures and create prettier results. The wire guide attaches to the presser foot or the shank (depending on your machine) and guides the yarn to the presser foot. The braiding foot has a shaped opening to feed the yarn perfectly to the needle and a wide groove on the underside to accommodate the yarn flowing under the presser foot. Specialty feet and accessories are available for all machine brands. Check with your dealer.

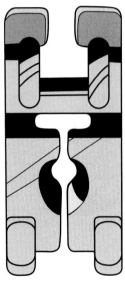

Braiding foot

Ombre Embroidered Scarf

Since both sides of the scarf will theoretically be the "right" side, use decorative thread in both the needle and the bobbin and a stabilizer that doesn't remain in the stitching.

Choose an embroidery design that is moderately stitch filled. You want enough fill stitches to showcase the decorative thread and the design but you don't want dense, heavily stitched motifs because the weight of the thread buildup can overpower the fleece and cause it to distort. Also, dense designs require a heavy cut-away stabilizer to maintain the integrity of the motif. You want no visible stabilizer remaining.

The embroidery motifs shown are from Viking design disk 100, which comes with the Designer 1 machine.

MATERIALS

Fleece: 1/3 yard

Embroidery sewing machine

Machine embroidery designs

40 wt. rayon thread for embroidery

Heavyweight water-soluble stabilizer

Lightweight water-soluble stabilizer (for topping)

Decorative rotary blade

DIRECTIONS

1. Trim the selvages but don't cut the scarf to the finished size yet.

2. Hoop the heavyweight water-soluble stabilizer.

3. Very lightly mist the stabilizer to make it tacky. Adhere the scarf end, centering it in the hoop.

4. Overlay the stitching area with lightweight water-soluble stabilizer and pin or baste it in place. (This will serve as a topping to ensure even thread coverage over the fleece nap.)

5. Embroider the design on your embroidery machine.

6. Remove the fabric and stabilizer from the hoop. Trim away as much stabilizer as possible.

7. Refer to the manufacturer's directions and soak the embroidered scarf to dissolve the stabilizer.

8. Use a decorative rotary blade to cut the scarf to size 11" x 60", centering the embroidery motif.

9. Shape the end of the scarf to complement the embroidery design.

Stitch Effects Scarf

Generally speaking, heat-set embellishments aren't appropriate for fleece. Because fleece is a napped synthetic fiber, heat and pressure frequently result in unattractive permanently flattened nap.

Heat-set embellishments require high heat and pressure. Combine those requirements with the size of the typical iron soleplate relative to the size of the embellishment being applied, and you can easily envision an affixed embellishment surrounded by an undesirable imprint of the soleplate.

The Clover Mini Iron is a great tool that allows you to take advantage of heat-set embellishments while lowering the risk of damaging the fleece surface. Once you know the danger, you can "cheat" to reduce the risk. With its tiny soleplate, the Mini Iron limits the heat and pressure to the embellishment area only, without endangering the surrounding fleece nap.

When choosing iron-on appliqués, transfers, and other heat-set embellishments, look for embellishments that don't require a long heat-set time, such as Stitch Effects Iron-On Transfers. The Stitch Effects directions instruct you to heat your iron to the cotton setting, place the transfer design side down (against the fabric), and iron each part of the design for 20 to 30 seconds. You can modify that procedure to make it suitable for fleece.

Instead of heat setting for a continuous 20 to 30 seconds, break it up into three 10-second increments. Keeping the Mini Iron soleplate in contact with *only the design backing* (never in direct contact with the fleece), press for 10 seconds, using tiny circular motions to avoid pressing in one place (and reducing the imprint danger.) Work your way around the entire design in 10-second increments until the entire motif has had one 10-second session.

Repeat two more times, for a total of 30 seconds… just not all at one time.

Because you did the heat set in increments, the bond is not quite complete. Carefully peel off the paper backing, overlay the design with a Teflon pressing sheet, and press as needed to finish the bonding. (Again,

keep the soleplate completely in the design area.)

Nancy's Hint
If the transfer directions require 40 or more seconds to adhere, it probably won't work well on fleece. Test it on a scrap first.

Sunshine Blanket

This cheerful blanket features blunt edge finish, blunt edge appliqué, and quick fringe bunny ears.

MATERIALS

Main fleece (blanket): 1 yard

White fleece (appliqué): ¼ yard

Yellow fleece (sunshine): ½ yard

Templates for Large and Medium Cloud and Bird on pages 155 to 157

Decorative edge rotary cutter

DIRECTIONS

1. Using a decorative rotary blade, cut a fleece blanket 36" x 45", gently rounding the corners.

2. Cut a 15" diameter circle from the yellow fleece.

3. Using a water-soluble pencil, draw a 13" circle centered inside the 15" circle on the right side of the yellow fleece.

4. Using the inner drawn circle for the beginning of the fringe, cut 2" long fringe, making the fringe cuts 1¼" wide at the base (the 13" circle line). Since you are working in a circle, the fringe cuts will fan out slightly, making them wider at the ends than the 1¼" beginning width.

5. Make the fringe into bunny ears. (Refer to page 106 for bunny ear instructions.)

6. Cut one large cloud, one medium cloud, and three birds from white fleece. (If you have an embroidery machine, embroider the words "You Are My Sunshine" using a satin stitch letter font on white fleece, then cut out the larger cloud, centering the words.)

7. Lightly spray temporary adhesive on the wrong sides of the sun, cloud, and bird appliqués and adhere them to the blanket. (Refer to the photo for placement.)

Nancy's Hint
I found it easiest to place the sun appliqué first, positioning it lower than the center of the blanket.

8. Stitch the sun to the blanket, sewing a skimpy ¼" inside the bunny ear slits.

9. Pin the bunny ear points to the blanket, creating a soft roll. Tack them in place by stitching a 2mm wide zigzag approximately ½" below the fringe point.

10. Edgestitch the cloud and bird appliqués to the blanket.

Southwest Throw

This throw and coordinating pillows have to be about the easiest and quickest way to freshen a room. The throw is simply quick fringed and finished with pony beads for a fun accent.

MATERIALS

Throw (54" x 60"): 1½ yards plus extra for appliqués for pillows

Blanket (60" x 72"): 2 yards plus extra for appliqués for pillows

6mm x 9mm pony beads: 2 gross

Fasturn tube turner or US9/1.25 metal crochet hook (to apply pony beads)

DIRECTIONS

1. Cut the fleece to the desired size.

2. Quick fringe two opposing ends of the throw. Make the fringe cuts a generous ½" to ⅝" wide x 5" long. (Refer to page 93 for quick fringe directions.)

Nancy's Note
Cut the fringe a little wider than ½" so it doesn't get distorted when you're beading the ends. Fringe cuts, especially those made on the crossgrain, will stretch when pulled through the bead holes.

3. Using a Fasturn or crochet hook, place the beads on the fringe. Tie the ends to secure. (Refer to page 110 for directions.)

Nancy's Note
Don't put beads on blankets or pillows that will be around small children. The beads aren't secure enough for curious minds, little hands, and busy fingers.

Southwest Pillows

Study your fleece print and determine what elements can be used for interesting appliqué motifs or accent bands. The throw print offered a variety of blunt edge appliqué options for the pillows. For maximum interest, vary the appliqué sizes and shapes, as well as the pillow sizes. Making the pillows "envelope style" allows you to easily change pillow covers for different seasons or holidays.

MATERIALS

Fleece main color solid (for pillow): ⅝ yard mid-weight fleece

Fleece contrast color (for fat piping): ⅛ yard

Fleece appliqués or accent bands cut from blanket fleece print

16" square pillow form

100/16 universal needle (for construction*)

Nancy's Note

These Materials and Directions are for a 16" pillow form. The requirements for different size pillow forms are given on page 141.

*Nancy's Note

Normally you would use a 14/90 needle for construction, but when you sew the fat piping, you will be stitching through three and four layers of fleece and will need the strength of the larger size needle.

DIRECTIONS

1. From contrast fleece color, cut one 3" x 60" trim strip for the fat piping edge finish.

2. From the main fleece color, cut one pillow front, 19" x 19" (3" larger than the pillow form) and cut two pillow half backs, 17½" x 12¾".

Nancy's Note

If you have enough fleece and nap or print is not an issue, cut the 17½" in the direction of the least stretch. Since you are making an envelope-style closing on the backside of the pillow, there is less potential for distortion if it is cut this way.

3. On the right side of the pillow front, arrange the fleece appliqués (or accent bands) as desired. Lightly spray the wrong side of the appliqués (or accent bands) with temporary adhesive spray and adhere them to the pillow front.

Nancy's Note

If your fleece print doesn't offer defined motifs for appliqués, make one up! It can be as simple as a geometric shape that complements the flavor of the print. Notice that most of the appliqués used on the Southwest Pillows are geometric shapes.

4. Stitch the appliqués (or accent bands) to the pillow front using one of the following methods.

a. Using regular thread in the needle and an edgestitch or edge-joining presser foot, edgestitch the appliqué in place.

b. With rayon thread in the needle, stitch the appliqués (or accent bands) in place. Choose a blanket stitch, lengthening and widening the stitch for a noticeable stitch. For an even bolder stitch, thread the machine with two spools of contrast rayon thread, threading both threads through the larger eye of the size 16/100 needle. Sew slowly to avoid thread loops.

5. Retrue and trim the pillow front to 17½" x 17½" (1½" larger than the pillow form).

Nancy's Note

Starting with a 19" x 19" pillow front, then trimming to 17½" x 17½" provides a fudge factor in case the appliqués are not centered exactly or something shifts during the stitching process.

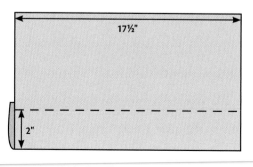

6. Turn under and topstitch 2" hems on one long edge of each half back.

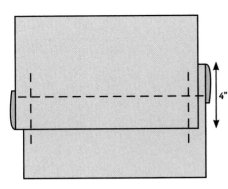

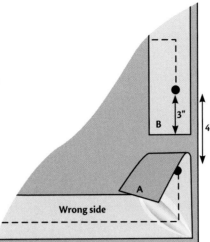

7. Overlap the half back hems 4" and baste them together with ¾" seam allowances.

8. Pin the pillow front to the basted pillow half backs with wrong sides together (finished position).

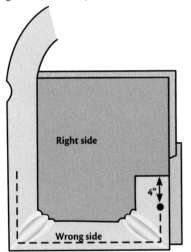

9. Place the right side of the 3" trim strip (from Step #1) against the right side of the pillow front.

10. Using an *exact* ¾" seam allowance, begin sewing 4" from the end of the trim strip. (You are sewing through three layers: front, back, and trim strip.) To avoid additional bulk when you splice the strip ends, begin stitching the trim strip away from the pillow back overlap area.)

11. Sew the trim strip to the outer edge of the pillow. Slightly stretch the trim strip while sewing. Pivot at the corners. Stop sewing exactly 4" before the beginning stitching.

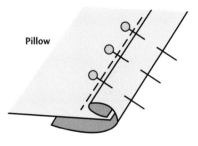

12. Cut the ending edge of the strip exactly 3" beyond the ending stitching.

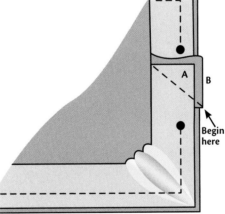

13. Lift up both unsewn ends of the trim strip. Match and pin edges as illustrated with right sides together.

Nancy's Hint
Pin first, check, then sew. It's easier to unpin than tear out stitching!

14. Sew A to B "on the diagonal," beginning exactly at the corner of B.

15. Before trimming the spliced strip, double check on the right side to make sure everything looks right. Trim the seam allowance to ¼" and finger press it open.

16. Finish sewing the last 4" of the spliced trim strip to the pillow.

17. Trim away one seam allowance layer in the *overlap area only* on the half

backs, to make the bulk comparable to the rest of the pillow. (Don't trim away any other seam allowance. In the following steps, when wrapping and enclosing the seam allowance, the fluffiness of the fleece "plumps" the wrap and gives a fat piping appearance.)

18. To finish the fat piping edge, wrap the trim strip to the backside, wrapping up, over, and around, to encase the raw edge of the seam allowances. Trim just the tips of the pillow corners for ease in wrapping.

[Image: Pillow with pins]

19. Working from the front of the pillow, pin the trim strip in place, making sure the plump wrapped edges are consistent.

20. Using an edgestitch or edge-joining presser foot for precise stitch placement, stitch in the ditch on the right side of the pillow to secure the wrapped trim strip. (To stitch in the ditch, sew exactly in the seamline.) Use needle thread that matches the main fleece color (pillow) and bobbin thread that matches the contrast color (fat piping).

21. On the backside of the pillow, use appliqué scissors to cut the excess trim close to the stitching line (page 65).

22. Insert the pillow form through the flap opening.
Optional: Attach a snap, button, or Velcro to hold the envelope back closed.

Kokopelli Throw

Side-by-side fringe cuts tied together add a slightly different edge finish. The coordinate pillow uses the fleece print for the blunt edge appliqué and fat piping pillow edge finish.

MATERIALS

Throw (54" x 60"): 1½ yards plus ⅛ yard for fat piping for 16" coordinate pillow

Blanket (60" x 72"): 2 yards plus ⅛ yard for fat piping for 16" coordinate pillow*

* Buy additional print fleece for appliqués

DIRECTIONS

1. Cut the fleece to the desired size.

2. Quick fringe two opposing ends of the throw. Make the fringe cuts a generous ½" wide x 5" long. (Refer to page 93 for quick fringe directions.)

3. Beginning at one corner, tie two side-by-side fringe cuts in a simple double knot.

Kokopelli Pillow/Multiple Pillow Sizes

The directions for construction are exactly the same as the Southwest Pillows on page 138 except the fat piping is made using the blanket fleece print. Contrast fleece yardages listed below are for the fat piping only. Purchase enough additional fleece print for the appliqués.

Follow the construction directions for the Southwest Pillows, adjusting for different pillow form sizes as follows:

20" Pillow Form

- Main yardage: ⅔ yard
- Contrast yardage: ¼ yard (for fat piping)
- Cut two contrast strips 3" x 60" long (for fat piping)
- Splice trim strips to make one long strip. (Refer to page 69 for directions)
- Cut the pillow front 23" x 23" (3" larger than pillow form)
- Cut two half backs 21½" x 14¾"
- Trim the pillow front to 21½" x 21½"

18" Pillow Form

- Main yardage: ⅝ yard
- Contrast yardage: ¼ yard (for fat piping)
- Cut two contrast strips 3" x 60" long (for fat piping)
- Splice trim strips to make one long strip. (Refer to page 69 for directions)
- Cut the pillow front 21" x 21" (3" larger than pillow form)
- Cut two half backs 19½" x 13¾"
- Trim the pillow front to 19½" x 19½"

14" Pillow Form

- Main yardage: ½ yard
- Contrast yardage: ⅛ yard (for fat piping)
- Cut one contrast strip 3" x 60" long (for fat piping)
- Cut the pillow front 17" x 17" (3" larger than pillow form)
- Cut two half backs 15½" x 11¾"
- Trim the pillow front to 15½" x 15½"

Nancy's Note

One 3" x 60" strip will make fat piping for a 14" or 16" pillow form. Two 3" x 60" strips, spliced, are needed for a pillow form 18" or larger.

Sweet Dreams Blanket

Using two fleece layers together makes a nice cozy blanket, but a thin layer of batting adds just a bit more character to the project and a bit more of a "quilted" look.

I was at a trade show when I first saw the Cambridge Marking System. I loved how it simplified marking a quilting design. (They offer a wide variety of quilting designs including geometrics, hearts, rainbows, anchors, tulips, and more.) The fabric template is full size, making the marking much easier.

If you can't find Cambridge Marking System patterns at your local fabric shop, see the Resources on page 150.

BLANKET MATERIALS

Print fleece: 1¼ yards

Coordinate print or solid fleece: 1¼ yards

Decorative rotary blade (wave or scallop)

Low loft polyester crib batting

Cambridge Marking System quilting template (or mark your own quilt design)

DIRECTIONS

1. Cut both fleece layers to 45" x 60".

2. Lay the batting on the wrong side of one layer and zigzag baste stitch (4mm wide x 4mm long) using a ¾" seam allowance to secure the batting to the fleece. (The zigzag stitch should be ¾" away from the fleece blanket edge, not necessarily at the edge of the batting. The excess batting will be trimmed later.)

3. Pin the fleece layers with wrong sides together, sandwiching the batting.

4. On one of the fleece layers, mark your chosen quilting design.

5. At each fabric mark, zigzag in place to tack the quilt.

6. Retrue the sides of the blanket if necessary.

7. Trim the batting close to the zigzag baste stitching.

8. Sew the blanket layers together using a ½" seam allowance.

9. Use a wave or scallop decorative blade and trim the blanket outer edge close to the stitching.

10. Remove the basting stitches.

Nancy's Hint

Quilt the fleece layers first and sew the outer edges second. That way, if the layers shift a little during the quilting process, the outer edges can be retrued before stitching the blanket perimeter.

Nancy's Note

Using the Cambridge Marking System, you simply lay the fabric template on the fleece blanket, mark the fabric through the design cutout holes, remove the template, and stitch the design, following your fabric markings.

I admit I cheated. Since my two blanket layers, batting, and template easily fit under the presser foot, I skipped the marking process. I simply pinned the template to the fleece, slipped the blanket and template under the presser foot, and sewed tacking stitches (zigzag in place) right through the template holes!

I realize I was tempting fate, risking fabric shifting, but since the quilting design was so simple, I went for it. If my chosen motif had been more complex, I would have done the fabric marking step as instructed by the manufacturer.

Machine Set-Up to "Cheat"

a. Drop the feed teeth.
b. Either dramatically lessen the pressure on the presser foot or use a presser foot that doesn't come in full contact with the fabric (a darning foot or embroidery machine embroidery foot).
c. Monitor to make sure you are staying on course — no fabric shifting, no template shifting.

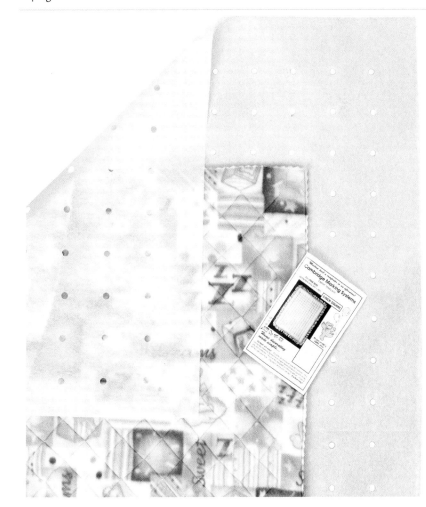

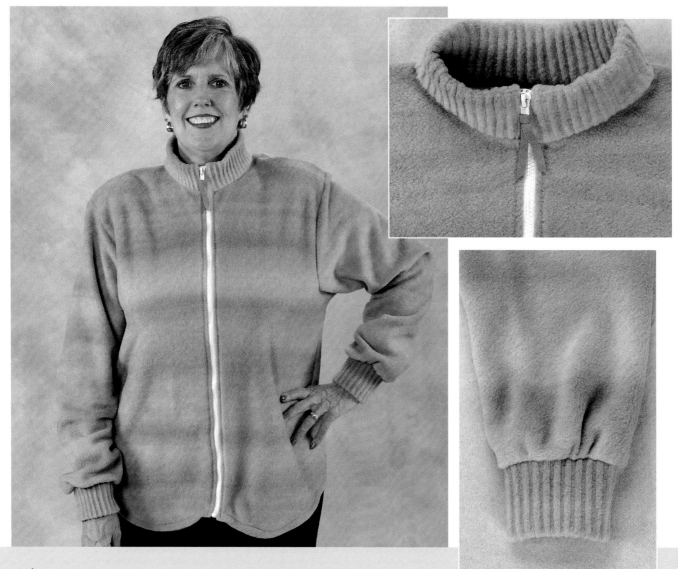

Chapter 8

Multi-Size Jacket Pattern - Fit Information and Construction

This moderately sized jacket is easy to construct, offers three lower hem finishes, three sleeve hem finishes, and a stand-up collar that can be left plain or polar ribbed. Choose any of the collar and hem options to make a plain jacket (like the pictured Ombre Jacket) or use the pattern as a base to make the Patchwork Jacket on page 26, the Trees Jacket on page 61, or the Jaguar Jacket on page 78. Or use the pattern as a "blank slate" to use a variety of embellishment techniques throughout the book.

Pattern Fit

When I make a garment I like to know beforehand how the pattern fits so I can adjust sizing for my particular shape and taste. Personally, I don't like a snug fit nor do I like a very oversized fit. I like a garment with moderate ease. With that in mind, I offer you the following information to help you determine how to use this multi-size master pattern to adapt for your personal taste.

The jacket has 10" to 12" bust ease for sizes S, M, and L. For XL the bust ease is 11" to 13".

For sizes S, M, and L, the hip ease is 8" to 10". For XL the hip ease is 9" to 11".

Note: *Greater ease measurements correspond to the smaller size in a size range. Lesser ease measurements correspond to the larger size in a size range.*

That means that if your bust measures 36" and your hip measures 38" and you make a size Medium, the finished garment will be 10" larger than your bust and 8" larger than your hips.

Refer to the charts for pattern sizing and finished measurements.

STANDARD BODY MEASUREMENTS

	S	M	L	XL
Bust	30"-32"	34"-36"	38"-40"	42"-44"
Hip	32"-34"	36"-38"	40"-42"	44"-46"

FINISHED GARMENT MEASUREMENTS

	S	M	L	XL
Bust & Hip	42"	46"	50"	55"

Using a Multi-Size Pattern

The beauty of a multi-size pattern is that most of us have multi-size bodies! Choose the jacket size according to your bust measurement. If your bust measures one size (let's say medium) and your hips measure a different size (let's be realistic here and say large), follow these instructions.

To preserve the multi-size master pattern for future use, overlay it with pattern tracing material (Do Sew, dotted tracing paper, or Quilter's Grid). Refer to page 21.

Trace the medium size bust, armscye, shoulder, neck, sleeve, and collar. Grade out to the large size for the hip area. Tracing in this manner adjusts the pattern to fit your shape (medium where you are medium, large where you are large), thus making a "personal pattern" for you, and keeping the master pattern intact for future use.

If you generally add sleeve length to a pattern, add length to this pattern accordingly. (You can always trim excess length before finishing the hem.)

Nancy's Hint

If you haven't considered a pattern's ease factors before and are not sure how they relate to fit, try this idea:

*Determine what pattern size you **think** you would make. Before cutting it out, measure a favorite similar style jacket that fits the way you would like this jacket to fit. Compare your favorite jacket's finished bust and hip garment measurement to this pattern's finished measurements in the size you chose. If there is a large discrepancy, choose the pattern size closest to your desired fit.*

Materials Needed

The information given below is for a basic jacket. It includes materials needed and construction directions for a basic jacket with the choice of:
- plain or polar-ribbed collar
- plain or polar-ribbed cuffs
- hemmed, elastic, or cuffed sleeves
- hemmed, elastic, or shirttail lower hem

For specific considerations or needs regarding the jacket variations featured in this book, see the page listed for that particular jacket (Jaguar Jacket page 78, Trees Jacket page 61, and Patchwork Jacket page 26).

If you lengthen the garment, increase the yardage needs and zipper length accordingly.

MATERIALS FOR BASIC JACKET

Fleece
  Small: 2 yards
  Medium: 2 yards
  Large: 2 yards
  Extra-large: 2 yards

Wash-Away Wonder Tape

Pattern tracing material

1" elastic (for elastic finish): 2 yards

Separating zipper
  Small and Medium: 28"
  Large and Extra-large: 30"

Cutting Directions: Cut Out Pattern Pieces "With Nap"

GARMENT BODY

Cut out two fronts and one back (on the fold), cutting the lower edge on the straight, shirttail, or elastic hem cutting line, as desired.

SLEEVES

Cut out two sleeves, cutting the lower edge on the straight, elastic, or cuffed cutting line, as desired.

COLLAR

Cut out one collar from plain fleece or "ribbed" yardage (see the polar ribbing yardage directions).

CUFFS

Cut out two cuffs from plain fleece or "ribbed" yardage (see the polar ribbing yardage directions).

While I did not include patch or side seam pockets in this pattern, you could easily "borrow" those pattern pieces and directions from a favorite pattern and include them during construction.

POLAR RIBBING YARDAGE

To make "ribbed" collar or cuffs, first cut a piece of fleece fabric larger than needed, sew rows and rows of pintucks to make the ribbing yardage, then cut the pattern pieces from ribbed fabric.

Cut from Fleece

1. For a polar ribbed collar, cut a piece of fabric 8" wide x 30" long, with the greater stretch in the length.

2. For polar ribbed cuffs, cut a piece of fabric 9" wide x 30" long with the greater stretch in the length.

Make the "Ribbing" Yardage

Using 4.0/100 or 6.0/100 double needles, and stitching on the right side of fabric, sew parallel rows of pintucks to entirely fill the fabric piece. Stitch the pintucks on the straight-of-grain, being careful to keep the rows as straight as possible. (To evenly space pintuck rows, align the right edge of the presser foot

along the previously sewn pintuck.) If there is a noticeable fabric nap, stitch with the nap.

Cut Out the Pattern Piece

Cut the pattern piece from the ribbed fabric. If the ribs are slightly offgrain, align the pattern straight-of-grain line to match the rib grain.

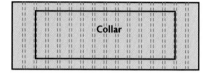

Nancy's Note

Handle the cut out ribbed piece gently, being careful not to stretch or pull the stitches. (For in-depth polar ribbing information, refer to my book, Polar Magic.)

General Sewing Directions

Note*: Use a ¼" seam allowance.*

SHOULDER SEAM

1. Before sewing the shoulder seams, embellish the garment front or back as desired (using techniques from the book or variations of your own).

2. With right sides together, sew the fronts to the back at the shoulder seam.

COLLAR

1. With right sides together, sew the collar to the neck edge, matching the ends of the collar to the jacket front edges and the midpoint of the collar to the center back.

2. Fold the collar in half lengthwise and mark the fold at both the center front edges with a pin.

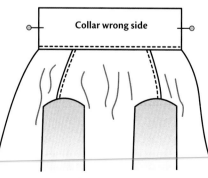

Jacket wrong side

ZIPPER

1. Place basting tape on the right side of the zipper along the outer edges of the zipper tape.

2. With right sides together, adhere the zipper to the front edge, placing the zipper bottom as follows:

For the topstitched straight hem : 1¾" from the lower edge.
For the encased elastic hem: 1¾" from the lower edge.
For the shirttail hem: ⅞" from the lower edge.

3. Stitch the zipper to the jacket, stopping the stitching at the pin-marked fold of the collar.

4. If necessary, fold the excess zipper tape (above the collar halfway mark) out of the way.

First side

Second side

5. Fold the collar right sides together, encasing the zipper. Stitch from the collar fold to the neck seamline. Stop at the neck seam, leaving ¼" inner collar seam allowance unstitched.

6. Topstitch the fronts from the lower edge to the neck seam, stitching ¼" away from the zipper.

7. Turn the collar to the finished position. Turn under the inner collar ¼" seam allowance and hand stitch to finish.

SLEEVES AND SIDE SEAMS

1. Before sewing the sleeve to the garment, embellish the sleeve as desired (using techniques from the book or variations of your own).

2. With right sides together, pin the sleeve to the armhole, matching the center of the sleeve to the shoulder seam and the garment armhole underarm points to the sleeve underarm points.

3. With the sleeve against the feed teeth and the garment on top, stitch the sleeve to the garment.

4. With right sides together, sew the front to the back, stitching from the lower hem edge up the side seam to the end of the sleeve.

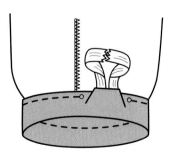

5. Finish sleeve hems as follows:

For the topstitched hem: Turn up 1¼" hem and topstitch it in place.

For the encased elastic hem: Turn up 1¼" hem and topstitch it in place, stitching close to the raw hem edge. Leave an opening to insert elastic. Cut elastic to the desired wrist fit and insert it in the opening. Overlap and stitch the ends to secure. Stitch the hem opening closed.

PLAIN OR POLAR RIBBED CUFF

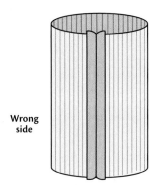

Wrong side

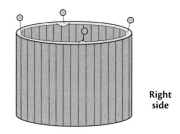

Right side

▲**1.** With wrong sides together, stitch each cuff, forming a circle.

▲**2.** Fold the cuff in half with wrong sides together. Divide the folded cuff into quarters and mark with pins.

3. Sew two rows of gathering stitches at the lower end of the sleeve. Stitch rows ¼" and ½" from the edge of the sleeve. Gather the sleeve to match the cuff.

▲**4.** With wrong sides together, sew the cuff to the gathered sleeve, being careful not to stretch or pull the pintuck stitches. If sewing with a conventional machine, stitch a second time slightly inside the first stitching.

GARMENT HEM FINISH

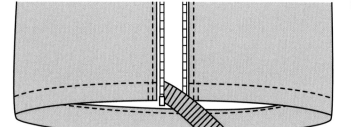

Finish the lower hem as follows:

For the topstitched straight hem: Turn up 1¼" hem and topstitch it in place.

◄*For the encased elastic hem*: Turn up 1¼" hem and topstitch it in place, stitching close to the raw hem edge. Insert the elastic and stitch it to secure at one center front hem opening. Pull the loose end of the elastic to the desired hip fit and pin and stitch it to secure. Trim the excess elastic.

For the shirttail hem: Turn up ⅝" hem and topstitch it in place, stitching close to the raw hem edge.

About the Author

Nancy Cornwell, also known as the "Polar Princess," has been an adventuresome sewer for over 35 years. She and her husband Jeff live in Seattle, Washington, where they golf, boat, and play bridge whenever Nancy isn't writing a new book, designing a pattern for the McCall Pattern Co., developing a magazine article, designing a new fleece line, taping television sewing programs, or traveling around the country giving seminars. (And that's on top of working full-time for David Textiles.)

Nancy and Jeff owned and operated a successful fabric store for 18 years. Their daughter Jackie and son Jeff grew up "in the business." Both are married and have gone on to launch successful business careers of their own. (Jackie is happily still in the fabric business.) Now Nancy and Jeff share their home with two cats, Molly and Ben, and mountains of fleece (waiting to be developed into a new ideas and techniques).

Today Nancy claims she has the best of both worlds: She works for the company that makes her favorite fleece, and her primary duty is to come up with more and more creative fleece ideas!

Nancy's love affair with fleece is obvious as you read through all of her books. She is passionate about creating and sharing new ideas, new ways of doing things, and developing new techniques. But most of all, Nancy's goal is to spark your imagination to use her ideas as a springboard for creativity in all your fleece sewing.

Resources

Support your local retailers. They work hard to bring you new fabrics, notions, books, patterns, machines, ideas, and classes. If you can't find what you want, let the store owners know what you are looking for. Support your local businesses and they will always be there for you.

Most of the products listed in this book are readily available at your local fabric or quilting store, or at your sewing machine dealer. If you can't find the products listed, refer to these companies.

Cactus Punch, Inc.
4955 N. Shamrock Place
Tucson, AZ 85705
(800) 487-6972
www.cactuspunch.com
Thousands of custom and original embroidery designs, plus a series of Signature Designs from well-known sewing industry experts.

Cambridge Marking System
Design Craft
8716 Sugarloaf Drive
Sandy, UT 84093
(801) 943-3720
Designer and manufacturer of fabric templates used for easy quilt marking.

Crowning Touch, Inc., The
3859 South Stage Road
Medford, OR 97501
(800) 729-0280
www.fasturnjunction.com
Designer and manufacturer of the Fasturn fabric tube turning system and patterns.

Kandi Corp.
PO Box 8345
Clearwater, FL 33758
(800) 985-2634
www.L-Orna.com
Manufacturers of the L'Orna Hot-Fix Applicator Wands, and specializing in hot-fix Swarovski crystals, pearls, nail heads, rhinestuds, and more.

Keiffer's
PO Box 719
Jersey City, NJ 07307
(201) 798-2266
If you can't find Lycra trim strips or nylon Lycra yardage (swimwear fabric) at your local fabric shop, Keiffer's is a good mail order source.

Krause Publications
700 E. State St.
Iola, WI 54990
(800) 258-0929
www.krause.com
Major publisher of sewing and hobby books.

Lyle Enterprises, Inc.
600 East Best Ave.
Coeur D'Alene, ID 83814
(800) 274-9193
www.lylefabrics.com
Mail order source for cotton/poly/Lycra ribbing (sold by the inch or yard), heavyweight cotton/poly/Lycra coat or jacket cuffs and bands (prepackaged), heavyweight nylon ribbing (sold by the inch), heavyweight nylon coat or jacket cuffs and bands (prepackaged), poly/cotton knit collars, and nonskid material for slipper soles.

Stretch & Sew, Inc.
PO Box 25306
Tempe, AZ 85285
(800) 547-7717
www.stretch-and-sew.com
Casual and sportswear multi-size patterns, Do-Sew pattern tracing material, Lycra trim strips and notions.

For reliable high-quality fleece prints and solids, look for the Nordic Fleece brand by David Textiles, Inc. on the bolt end.

Templates

Leaf

Paw Prints

Small Flower

Medium Flower

Large Flower

Leaf and Vine

Small Posy

Medium Posy

Large Posy

Snowflake #1

Crusher Hat/Scarf Flower

Snowflake #2

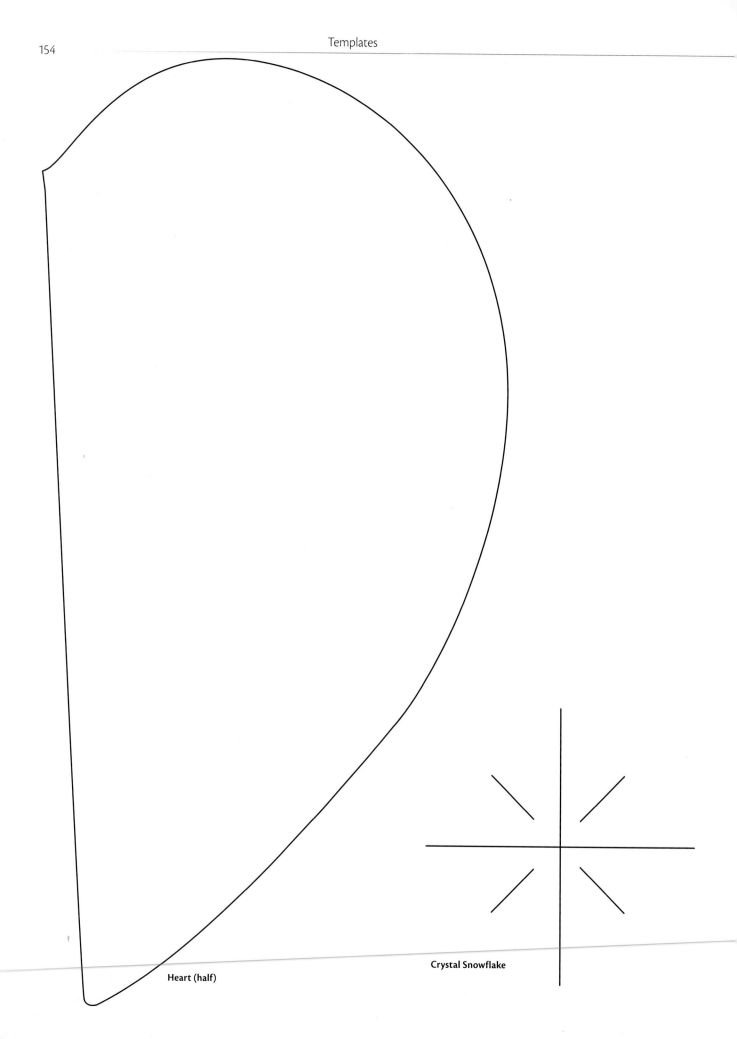

Heart (half)

Crystal Snowflake

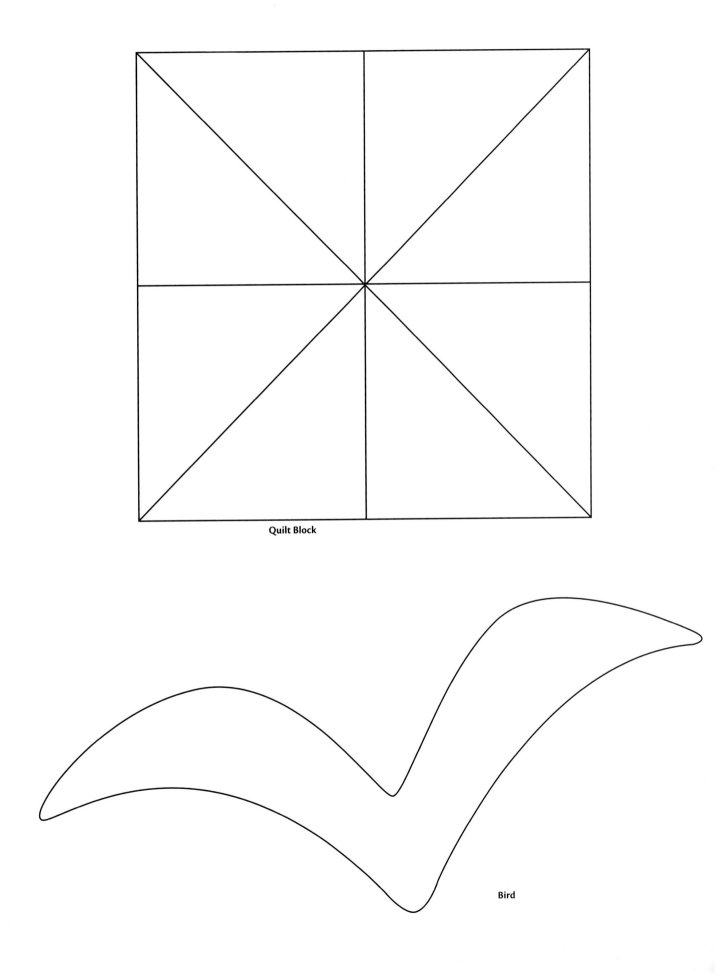

Quilt Block

Bird

Large Cloud (half)

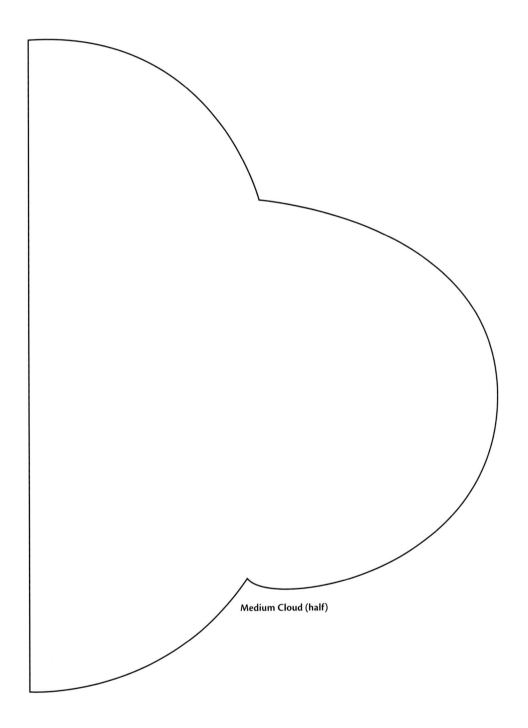

Medium Cloud (half)

Index

Adhesive spray, 19

Adventures With Polarfleece, 11, 17

Basting tape, 11

Blanket

    baby, 116

    double-layer, 30, 98, 99

    horse motif, 52

    no-sew, 100

    quilted panel, 126

    single-layer, 96, 97

    sunshine, 134

    sweet dreams, 142

Blunt edge finish, 30

    appliqué methods, 40-42

    armholes, 32

    collars or cuffs, 31

    crusher hat, 59

    double-sided appliqué methods, 43-44

    embellishment, 32

    horse appliqué pillow, 53

    horse motif blanket or throw, 52

    mittens, 32

    pockets, 31

    reversible jacket, 33

    reversible shawl collar jacket, 56

    reversible vest, 55

    scarf, 60

    snowflake reverse appliqué scarf, 62

    yoke lapped seams, 31

Boa, 107, 108

Chacopel pencil, 18

Cheater's binding, 35

Cheater's mitered corners, 35

Cheater's narrow self-fabric binding, 36

Cheater's wide self-fabric binding, 38

Cheater's wrapped edge, 64-65

    finished width, 67

    hat, 70

    no-side-seam vest, 70

    pillows, 71

    trim choices, 66-67

Chenille, 72

    appliqué, 87

    basket weave scarf, 80

    diamond chenille scarf, 82

    faux chenille, 73

    fleece chenille basics, 73

    hat, 90

    jacket, 78, 89

    robe, 83

    scarf, 89, 90

    strips, 76

    tote, 85

    yardage, 76

Clover Mini Iron, 14, 21

Crusher hat and scarf, 113

Cutting mats, 19

Decorative edge, 24, 26

Double-layer blankets and scarves, 30

Dritz electric scissors, 20

Drying, 13

Embroidery Machine Essentials, Fleece Techniques, 17

Fleece yarn, 48

    knitted fleece, 50

    laced edge, 49

    scalloped, 130

Hats,

    chenille, 113

    cheater's wrapped edge, 70

    crusher, 59, 90

Holmberg, Nanette, 73

Jacket

    chenille, 89

    jaguar, 78

    multi-size pattern fit information and

construction, 144

    patchwork, 26

    reversible, 33, 56

    trees, 61

Kellogg, Gail, 130

Laundering, 13

Mesh transfer canvas, 18

Mini iron, 14, 21

Mittens, 32

More Polarfleece Adventures, 17

Needles, 14-15

    size, 12

    type, 12

Olfa blades, 20

Omnistrip cutting mats, 19

Patchwork

    jacket, 26

    scarf, 24

Pattern tracing material, 21

Pencils, 18

Pillow

    cheater's wrapped edge, 71

    horse appliqué, 53

    kokopelli, 141

    no-sew, 102

    quilter's, 128

    Southwest, 137

Pins, 18

Polar Magic, 17

Pressing, 13

Pretreating, 13

Quick fringe, 92-93

    beaded vest and scarf, 110

    boa, 107, 108

    bunny ears baby blanket, 105

    double-layer blanket, 98, 99

    double-layer scarf, 95

    no-sew blanket, 100

    no-sew pillow, 102

    rag quilt, 103

    single-layer blanket, 96, 97

    single-layer scarf, 94

Quilt

    patchwork embroidered, 124

    rag, 103

Reverse appliqué, 45

Reverse hem, 34-39

Right side vs. wrong side, 14

Robe, chenille, 83

Rotary cutters, 20

Scarf

    basket weave, 80

    beaded, 110

    blunt edge, 60

    chenille, 89, 90

    crystal snowflake, 120

    diamond chenille, 82

    double-layer, 30, 95

    ombre embroidered, 132

    patchwork, 24

    single-layer, 94

    snowflake reverse appliqué, 62

    stitch effects, 133

Scissors

    appliqué, 20

    electric, 20

Stabilizer, 14

Stiletto, 21

Stitch length

    for sewing fleece, 10

    for sewing Lycra, 11

Sulky KK2000 adhesive spray, 19

Thread, 14

Throw

    kokopelli, 140

    Southwest, 136

Tote, chenille, 85

Vest

    beaded, 110

    no-side-seam, 70, 121

    reversible, 55

Wash-Away Wonder Tape, 11, 18

Yardage, 15